The Battle OF
Musgrove's Mill
1780

SMALL BATTLES

*Mark Edward Lender and James Kirby Martin, Series Editors*

*The Battles of Connecticut Farms and Springfield, 1780*
*by Edward G. Lengel*

*The Battle of Gloucester, 1777*
*by Garry Wheeler Stone and Paul W. Schopp*

*The Battle of Harlem Heights, 1776*
*by David Price*

*The Battle of Upper Sandusky, 1782*
*by Eric Sterner*

# The Battle OF Musgrove's Mill

# 1780

"Picked Men Well Mounted"

## JOHN BUCHANAN

SMALL
BATTLES

WESTHOLME
Yardley

Westholme Publishing, LLC
904 Edgewood Road
Yardley, Pennsylvania 19067
Visit our Web site at www.westholmepublishing.com

ISBN: 978-1-59416-393-7
Also available as an eBook.

Printed in the United States of America.

*You may not be interested in war,*
*but war is interested in you.*

*Attributed to Leon Trotsky*

# Contents

*Maps*

*A gallery of illustrations follows page 38*

# Series Editors' Introduction

WE ALL HAVE HEARD and likely read about the big battles of the American Revolution. Names like Trenton, Saratoga, and Yorktown resonate in our ears. But what about all the smaller battles that took place by the hundreds, often fought away from but related to the bigger battles. It is the contention of this series that these smaller actions, too often ignored, had as much impact, if not more, in shaping the outcomes of the American War of Independence.

These engagements were most often fought at the grassroots level. They did not directly involve His Majesty's professional forces under the likes of Generals William Howe, John Burgoyne, and Henry Clinton, or Continentals under Generals George Washington, Nathanael Greene, or Horatio Gates for that matter. Such smaller battles involved local forces, such as patriot militia and partisan bands of Loyalists, or at times Native Americans, mostly, but not always, fighting on the British side.

Quite often the big names were not there in such smaller-scale combat. Private Joseph Plumb Martin, writing in his classic memoir, recalled his fighting at Forts Mifflin and Mercer during November 1777. He and his comrades were trying to block British war and supply vessels moving up the Delaware River from reaching the king's troops under Sir William Howe who had captured Philadelphia. Had they prevailed and cut off this obvious supply route, Howe might well have had to abandon the city. But no, they did not succeed. Superior British firepower finally defeated these courageous American fighters.

What bothered Martin, besides so many good soldiers being seriously wounded or killed, was not the failed but valiant effort to cut off Howe's primary supply line. Rather, writing thirty years later, what particularly irked him was that "there has been but little notice taken of" this critical action. Martin was sure he knew why: "The reason of which is, there was no Washington, Putnam, or Wayne there. . . . Such [circumstances] and such troops generally get but little notice taken of them, do what they will. Great men get great praise, little men, nothing."

While Martin's blunt lament is unusual in the literature of the Revolution, the circumstances he described and complained of are actually fairly obvious. Although often brutal, the smaller engagements too frequently have received short shrift in popular narratives about the conflict. Nor have the consequences of these various actions been carefully studied in relation to the bigger battles and the outcomes of the War for Independence more generally. Small battles accounted for the lion's share of the combat that occurred during the American Revolution. The purpose of this series is to shine a bright new light on these smaller engagements while also getting to know those lesser persons who participated in them and grappling with the broader consequences and greater meaning of these actions on local, regional, and nation-making levels.

In the end, a more complete understanding of the Revolutionary War's big picture will emerge from the small-battles volumes that make up this series. If, as recent scholarship tells us, local history "allows us to peer deep into past societies and to see their very DNA," the Small Battles Series will do the same for the American War of Independence.

We are delighted to introduce *The Battle of Musgrove's Mill, 1780*, by John ("Jack") Buchanan, one of the true authorities on the War for Indepedence in the American South. If ever a small battle reflected the desperation of the revolutionary struggle in the South, Musgrove's Mill surely was it. The enagement took place on August 19, 1780, in western South Carolina. It pitted patriot militia against Loyalist militia and provincial regulars, and was thus an "all-American" affair—part of the brutal civil war that plagued the rebellious colonies. It was a brief but bloody fight, in fact one of the bloodiest of the war considering the numbers involved; and Buchanan has situated the battle in the context of personalities—much depended on who commanded Rebel and Loyalist forces—and the on-going wider war. Indeed, Musgrove's Mill took place within days of the devastating American defeat at Camden, but also in the run-up to the Rebel triumph at King's Mountain, where the men who fought on August 19 helped smash Major Patrick Ferguson's Loyalists. Buchanan sagely observes that had Ferguson paid greater attention to the events at Musgrove's Mill, he might have thought twice about his challenge to the Rebel "Over Mountain" militia. A full account of the engagement at Musgrove's Mill and its implications has long been over-due, and we are fortunate that John Buchanan has told the story with such insight and verve. *The Battle of Musgrove's Mill, 1780* will now stand as the authoritative history of this remarkable action.

Mark Edward Lender
James Kirby Martin
Series editors

# Preface

THE BATTLE OF MUSGROVE'S MILL was one of some 213 engagements that peppered South Carolina in the years 1775–1782, during the eight-year Revolutionary War (the longest American war
until the Vietnam War). Musgrove's Mill, however, is of unique
interest because it led directly to a battle that had a game-changing impact on the Revolutionary War—a significance largely unrecognized.

The battle also encompasses the story of three remarkable
men who drove the action. And they did it acting as a single command head. A keen student of the Southern Campaign, Brigadier
General George Fields (ret.), wrote, "It certainly is one of few, if
not the only battle, won by a committee." In fact, a participant in
the enterprise referred to the command structure as "conjoint,"
for there was no overall commander. Yet I have seen no evidence
of differences between the Colonels, who worked together as a
well-oiled team. How sad that these heroes of the Revolution are
unknown today. It is high time to shed light on Colonel Elijah
Clarke, Colonel Isaac Shelby, and Colonel James Williams.[1]

Thus when Mark Lender paid me the honor of inviting me to contribute a volume to the Small Battle Series, I chose the Battle of Musgrove's Mill because I wanted not only to tell the story of the battle and its significance but also the stories of the Colonels, their lives before Musgrove's Mill, their lives afterward. What had they done before the battle that qualified them to lead men on a desperate venture? How did they behave in action? Did they survive the war? After eight years of war, how did they handle peace? This volume, therefore, is about the Colonels as much as the important battle in which they were "conjoint."

As a battle, Musgrove's Mill stands out not only for its significance but also the dire situation in which the 200 Rebel militiamen found themselves before the fighting began. Worn out from an all-night ride, their horses blown and unable to go farther, believing that somewhere behind them were some 1,000 Loyalist militia and regulars, the united partisans from North Carolina, South Carolina, and Georgia found themselves facing, to their surprise, a numerically superior enemy, including American regulars serving the British cause. Leadership and tactics would tell the tale as the enemy closed on the Rebel position. The Rebels' physical toughness, previous fighting experience, and familiarity with the weapons they carried certainly played a role in the battle. There was, however, something else involved that inspired these part-time fighting men to undertake a precarious venture. A feeling within Rebel militia time after time led them to put their lives on the line. It was called freedom. Not the phony variety about vaccines and masks bandied about in our time of pandemic, but freedom as expressed by a Rebel named Daniel Collins as quoted by his sixteen-year-old son James, who rode off to war with his father. Daniel came home from viewing the ruins of Billy Hill's iron works, which Back Country farmers relied upon. It had been burned to the ground by Captain Christian Huck and a detachment of the British Legion, American regulars serving with the British army. Daniel's wife Elizabeth asked him for the news.

"Nothing very pleasant. I have come home determined to take my gun and when I lay it down, I lay down my life with it; then, turning to me said, my son, you may prepare for the worst; the thing is fairly at issue. We must submit or become slaves, or fight. For my part I am determined—tomorrow I will go to join Moffit."[2]

A NOTE ON TERMINOLOGY AND SOURCES

I use the language of the time, what enemies in this first American civil war called each other. I prefer Rebels for the American revolutionaries. That is what the British and Americans loyal to King George called them, and that is what they were: Rebels against constituted authority—until they won the war. The Rebels called themselves Whigs, after the British political party that was then out of power, but that word is so . . . well, dull, and for me has a humorous connotation. Supporters of the king called themselves Loyalists and many historians use that term. With a few exceptions, I prefer Tory, because that is what the Rebels called them. I also prefer Musgrove's Mill as opposed to Musgrove Mill, even though the latter is the official spelling used by the State of South Carolina at the Musgrove Mill Historic Site. Participants in the battle and other contemporaries spelled it Musgrove's.

In writings the Rebel militia of the Southern Back Country have also been called partisans since their time to the present day. In the military sense, partisan means a guerilla band operating within enemy lines, which is exactly what the Rebel militia bands were. (Partisan was also used then for regulars operating as light troops on the flanks, rear, and van of an army, guarding against surprise and engaging in forays against the enemy.) I use partisan and militia interchangeably.

Provincial regulars (or provincials) were Americans loyal to George III. They were raised, outfitted, trained, armed, and paid in the manner of British regulars.

I always keep to the original spellings and punctuations in correspondence. Readers will not find the annoying [*sic*] in this story.

There are four firsthand Rebel accounts of the Battle of Musgrove's Mill, but only one is contemporary. One of our Colonels, James Williams, wrote an official report on September 5, 1780, seventeen days after the battle (Graves, Appendix 9, 196–97), which he delivered to Major General Horatio Gates in Hillsborough, North Carolina. It is spare, the length of a printed page, but written when his memory was fresh. Colonel Elijah Clarke, who could neither read nor write, surely spoke to others about the battle, but if so his recollections are either not extant or have yet to surface. Our third Colonel, Isaac Shelby, wrote a more detailed account—but in 1814, thirty-four years after the battle (Graves, Appendix 15, 227–30 for readers, although I have used another source). I have accepted some of Shelby's account, rejected other parts. The fullest account is by Lieutenant Colonel Samuel Hammond (1757–1842), who served under Colonel Williams. Hammond's account did not appear in transcription until 1851 in Joseph Johnson, *Traditions and Reminiscences Chiefly of the American Revolution in the South* . . . . (Graves, 102–4, n. 208). Some historians have rejected it because the original has never appeared. It has the ring of truth to me, however, and for the most part I accept it. Hammond also referred to his participation at Musgrove's Mill in his 1832 pension application (Graves, 105–6). Our fourth primary source, Major Joseph McJunkin (1755–1846), gave Musgrove's Mill brief mention in his 1833 pension application, a fuller account in a narrative he dictated in 1837 to his grandson-in-law, and a Statement (Graves, Appendix 17, 267–320). McJunkin is off on many details, thus I have relied on it sparingly. I have also read several pension applications of militiamen who fought at Musgrove's Mill and quoted from some of them. With these applications, one must always keep in mind that they were very old men when they gave sworn testimony, for militiamen or their widows were only included in the supplementary Pension Act of 1832. Having turned ninety a few months before writing this, I can sympathize with them when they err or confuse matters. At their best, however, the pension applications are good evidence and add drama to events. The only firsthand British account that has so far appeared is a brief paragraph by the famous Tory David Fanning in his postwar narrative. There is limited information in diaries of provincial regulars and official British correspondence that will be described in the chapter on the battle and its aftermath.

---

Now, LET US BEGIN THE STORY of Musgrove's Mill by first setting the stage in the Deep South in 1780, and then introducing the Colonels.

# ONE

# "Pack of Beggars"

SOUTH CAROLINA LAY PROSTRATE under the British boot. An expeditionary force of 8,500 British and German regulars under the commander in chief of British forces in America, General Sir Henry Clinton (1730–1795), had landed in South Carolina on February 11, 1780, moved steadily over the barrier islands and through the wetlands of the Low Country against little opposition, and gradually tightened a noose around the citadel of the Rice Kings. The surrender of Charleston on May 12, 1780, and with it the only American army in the South, shocked Low Country Rice Kings, who had overcome Tory resistance and controlled South Carolina since 1775. Some Low Country nabobs who valued property before honor flocked to the conqueror and signed a craven document of loyalty to the Crown. And later some leading Back Country Rebel militia commanders took parole.[1]

The British had been thinking of a Southern offensive since 1775. Among the messages from America that beguiled the government in London were reports from royal governors in exile and American Tories that, upon the appearance of a British army, hordes of Americans loyal to Britain were ready to rise in the southern Back Country. Lord George Germain, who ran the war from London as Secretary of State for America, was especially taken in by such reports. In Georgia "There are still many friends to government here," wrote Sir James Wright in 1775. In the same year in South Carolina, Lord William Campbell passed on a report from a Back Country Tory leader that 4,000 Loyalists awaited British support to arm themselves. In 1775 Josiah Martin of North Carolina promised 20,000 ready to support the king's authority, although a year later he reduced that number to 9,000. In truth, the Tories were in the minority in the southern Back Country. Later in the narrative we will look at the numbers in South Carolina, which became the main theater of war in the Deep South.[2]

There were also Indian allies to consider. Indians throughout the country knew that an American victory would unleash hordes of land-hungry whites who had no respect for treaties establishing lines between settlers and Indians. From the beginning most Indians had thrown in their lot with Great Britain. In the South Cherokee, Creek, Choctaw, and Chickasaw outnumbered whites, but only the Cherokee and Creek Nations were close enough for the chance to play an important role for the British. Although qualms existed among ministers and members of Parliament in London about unleashing Indian wars, General Thomas Gage, then British commander in chief in America, had no reservations on that score: "We must not be tender of calling upon the Savages," he wrote to Lord Dartmouth in June 1775. Lieutenant General Charles, 2nd Earl Cornwallis (1738–1805) thought otherwise. In early July 1780, he wrote to Lieutenant Colonel Nisbet Balfour, "I beg you will explain to Colonel [Thomas "Burntfoot"] Brown in the most positive manner that I wish to keep the Indians in good humour, but on no account whatever to bring them forward or employ them." After receiving a letter from Colonel Brown on the importance of the Indians, his Lordship wrote directly to Brown. "I should desire that they be kept in good humour . . .

but I would on no account employ them on any operations of war." The British never employed the southeastern Indians in a meaningful way. When the Cherokee engaged in a major offensive in 1776 without British support—aside from munitions—American retaliation was swift and devastating. An American militia offensive into Indian country knocked the Cherokee out of the war for four years. A minor Cherokee rising in 1781 was quickly defeated, and the Creek Nation never brought its full strength to bear in the service of the British. As early as 1776, John Stuart, British Superintendent of Indian Affairs in the South, reported that "all the Southern Tribes are greatly dispirited, by the unopposed successes of the Rebells, and no appearance of any Support from Government to His Majesties distressed subjects in the interior parts of the Provinces, or to the Indians who have engaged in His Majesty's cause." The frontier and Back Country continued to suffer solitary raids, often by mixed parties of Indians and Tories. But unlike the Iroquois in New York State, the Southeastern Indians were not a significant factor in the war.[3]

Nor were slaves. Of the 104,000 slaves in South Carolina, all but 10 percent were in the Low Country where they vastly outnumbered whites. Upon the arrival of a British army in 1780 thousands flocked to British lines. But the British made use of few as soldiers. The great majority continued to work the Low Country rice and indigo plantations. Both sides also used slaves as laborers. And the argument by some historians that the South rebelled to protect slavery is pure fiction.[4]

Following the drawn Battle of Monmouth at Monmouth Court House, New Jersey, in the summer of 1778, the war in the North was stalemated. After three years of war and major battles, including the loss of an entire British army at Saratoga in New York State, Albion's attempt to subdue the northern states had failed. There would be no more grand battles north of Mason-Dixon. To make matters worse for Britain, in March 1778 France became an ally of the American Rebels. For Britain, the war to subdue the Rebels became a world war, and among the dangers were loss of her valuable sugar islands in the West Indies. Bases south of

Mason-Dixon would make it easier to protect their West Indian colonial empire from French attempts at conquest, provide supplies to British forces in the islands, and perhaps present opportunities to pick off French sugar islands. Finally, after five years of considering it, the British had moved south.

Although an extended discussion of British southern strategy is well beyond the scope of this book, it should be emphasized again that by the summer of 1778 the government in London had given up on subduing the northern colonies. As commander in chief, it was General Sir Henry Clinton's duty to carry out the southern strategy. Sir Henry was an intelligent strategist. His decision to concentrate on South Carolina was correct. Had it been followed successfully—and of course that is a big *if*—the possibility existed of the war ending with a negotiated settlement that left South Carolina, Georgia, the Floridas (the latter then including large parts of southern Alabama and Mississippi), and the vast country between the Appalachian Mountains and the Mississippi River as British possessions. Sir Henry's deputy, Lieutenant General Cornwallis, who took command of the Southern Theater when Sir Henry returned to New York, was a bold commander and a competent eighteenth-century tactician. In battle, Cornwallis always knew where he belonged in a crisis—up front with the troops. But he was not an intelligent strategist. His Lordship would ruin Sir Henry's plans by leaving South Carolina, marching north, and after many adventures ending up in Virginia where he met his Waterloo and lost America. That tale, as fascinating as it is, also exceeds our purpose.[5]

To return to the situation in South Carolina in the early summer of 1780, all seemed to be going well. Some three weeks after Charleston fell, a triumphant Sir Henry Clinton wrote to Cornwallis, "From every information I receive, and numbers of the most violent rebels hourly coming in to offer their services, I have the strongest reason to believe the general disposition of the people to be not only friendly to Government but forward to take up arms in its support." Cornwallis replied, "Appearances in this province are certainly very favorable." Yet nine days later, June 7,

1780, Lieutenant Colonel Nisbet Balfour (1743–1823) reported otherwise. Balfour had left Charleston on May 26, with a force of about 600 British and provincial regulars: a detachment of Light Infantry, three companies of 7th Foot, Prince of Wales American Regiment, and Major Patrick Ferguson's American Volunteers. Balfour was on his way to take command of the far Back Country village of Ninety Six, 175 miles northwest of Charleston, and 32 miles south of Musgrove's Mill. Ninety Six began as an Indian trading post: European goods for the hides of the whitetail deer. In June 1780 it consisted of twelve houses, a courthouse, and a jail. It would soon be protected by a fort and become the main British outpost in the far Back Country. Its name came from the belief that it was ninety-six miles northwestward to the Cherokee town of Keowee on the south bank (some say west) of the Keowee River. It was closer to eighty-one miles. The site of Keowee is now under Lake Keowee.[6]

About halfway on his march, June 2, 1780, Balfour wrote to Lord Cornwallis, "I have used my best endeavors to find out proper people for militia officers in this and other districts, but I cannot find a single man of any property or consequence that has not been of Rebel service, and from the Congarees to Neilson's (Nelson's) Ferry is a very disafected and populous district." On June 12, however, Balfour wrote that while "it will be absolutely necessary to have a post here," he believed "From every appearance I am allmost certain of no resistance from the Back Country." Yet twelve days later he reported from Ninety Six, "Things are by no means in any sort of settled state, nor are our friends, so numerous as I have suspected, from Saluda to Savannah River. Almost the whole district . . . are disaffected and althow at present overawed by the presence of the troops, yet are ready to rise on the smallest change. As to their disarming it is a joke; they have given in only old useless arms and keep their own good ones." So which was it? Resistance or not from the Rebels? The British would bounce from optimism to pessimism and back.[7]

About the time Sir Henry Clinton wrote optimistically to Cornwallis, an incident occurred that would have an electric impact on opinion in the Back Country. Colonel Abraham Buford (1747–1833) had been marching southward toward Charleston with a 350-strong Continental unit (3rd Virginia Detachment). When the city fell, Buford began retiring northward. Sir Henry, planning to return to New York, gave Cornwallis the task of pacifying the rest of South Carolina and establishing strongpoints. Cornwallis' initial goal was Camden, South Carolina, on the same road taken by Buford. He ordered twenty-six-year-old Lieutenant Colonel Banastre Tarleton (1754–1833) to pursue Buford. Tarleton commanded the British Legion, a provincial regular unit of horse and foot formed in the North in 1778 by merging three Loyalist units—Philadelphia Light Dragoons, Caledonian Volunteers, Kinloch's Light Dragoons— and the following year absorbing the Bucks County Light Dragoons, as well as drafting men from various Loyalist units. Many of the men were from New York, New Jersey, and Pennsylvania. Attached to his command were about forty to fifty troopers of the British 17th Light Dragoons.[8]

Banastre Tarleton had grave defects of character in both war and peace. It is alleged, and I believe it, that "vanity" was his "prevailing foible." In America he failed to keep his British Legion in check. Even Tories were fair game for his men. According to the Philadelphia Tory Charles Stedman, during the siege of Charleston troopers of either the Legion or 17th Light Dragoons "attempted to ravish" three women, two of them Tories. The women were, wrote Lieutenant Anthony Allaire of the American Volunteers, "most shockingly abused" at Monck's Corner north of the city. Stedman, who was Cornwallis' commissary, stated that Ann Fayssoux, "a most delicate and beautiful woman," wife of Peter Fayssoux, Surgeon General of the Southern Continental Army, "was most barbarously treated." The trooper's choice of at least one victim was unwise. One of the Tory women was the widow of a prominent Tory, Sir John Colleton. Major Patrick Ferguson, whom we will discuss later, wanted the men executed. Stedman believed that they were taken to Charleston and "afterwards tried and whipped." Word of the outrages percolated to the top. Cornwallis wrote to Tarleton, "I must recommend to you

in the strongest manner to use your utmost endeavours to prevent the troops under your command [fro]m committing irreg-
ularities, and I am convinced that my recommend[atio]n will
have weight when I assure you that such conduct will [be hi]ghly
agreeable to the Commander in Chief." Upon Tarleton's return
to England after the war, Horace Walpole remarked that "Tarleton boasts of having slain more men and lain with more women
than anybody else in the army." Whereupon Richard Brinsley
Sheridan, who had known Tarleton before the war, responded,
"Lain with! What a weak expression! He should have said rav-
ished. Rapes are the relaxation of murderers." Tarleton lived for
several years with the actress Mary Robinson, known as Perdita,
after her most famous role. She had been intended for the Prince
of Wales' bed, but he had a change of heart and passed her on to
Tarleton. According to the diarist Joseph Farrington, she "separated from Tarleton on account of his designs on her daughter,
who is now 21." In the words of a noted historian in correspondence to the author, Tarleton was a "world-class cad." As a soldier,
however, Banastre Tarleton was formidable.[9]

Buford had a ten-day lead. The heat of the Carolina summer
was already oppressive, but Tarleton, ruthless driver of men and
horses, in hot pursuit was a man possessed. He started with 270
horsemen, his British Legion infantry also mounted. When he
caught up with Buford's 350-man regiment at the Waxhaws, a few
miles south of the North Carolina line, he had 160 men with him.
Behind was a trail of dead horses and men on foot who couldn't
keep up.

Tarleton had sent Captain David Kinlock ahead with a message
to Colonel Buford that vastly exaggerated his numbers and demanded Buford's surrender. Buford replied, "Sir, I reject your
proposals, and shall defend myself to the last extremity," which
fit perfectly the old saying, "famous last words." On May 29, 1780,
at 300 yards, Tarleton's cavalry and infantry "advanced to the
charge." In an appalling blunder, Buford ordered his infantry not
to fire until the enemy was ten yards away, time for only one volley. Tarleton's horse was killed under him and he and a few other

officers and troopers went down. But the mass of horsemen crashed into the Virginians and rode them down, or, as Tarleton wrote, the Virginia regiment "was completely broken, and slaughter was commenced."[10]

Since that day in 1780 the charge has been made that the fighting that lasted minutes was followed by a massacre of helpless men after a white flag had been raised. Recently, some writers have denied that a massacre happened. I believe it did, but there is no reason for us to get entangled in arguments for and against. The charge of massacre is strengthened by Tarleton himself. He wrote in his postwar memoir that the belief that "they had lost their commanding officer . . . stimulated the soldiers to a vindictive asperity not easily restrained."[11]

But whether Tarleton's force engaged in a massacre is irrelevant. The Rebels believed they had. Tarleton's reputation never recovered. He became the most hated man in the South, known far and wide as Bloody Tarleton and Bloody Ban. On many a southern battlefield echoed cries of "Buford, Buford," and "Tarleton's Quarter," as Rebels took vengeance. A bloody example will suffice. On February 25, 1781, Moses Hall, a twenty-one-year-old North Carolina militiaman, was taken to see Tory prisoners. "We went to where six were standing together. Some discussion taking place, I heard some of our men cry out, 'Remember Buford,' and the prisoners were immediately hewed to pieces with broadswords."[12]

Between the surrender of Charleston and June 5, British forces fanned westward into the Back Country, established forts along the Santee and Congaree Rivers to protect their lines of communication and supply; major bases at Camden in the mid-Back Country; Ninety Six in the far Back Country; Augusta just across the Savannah River in Georgia; and smaller strongpoints that completed the Back Country arc. Thereafter, when the main British army moved northward, control of South Carolina and Georgia would largely rest with the Tory militia.

Yet events in Georgia the previous year did not augur well for dependence upon Tory allies. The British invaded, took Savannah, marched into the Back Country, and occupied the frontier entrepot of Augusta on the Savannah River. It was the first stage in the reconquest of Georgia and South Carolina. The occupying force in Augusta consisted of only about 1,000 British and provincial regulars. How were the British expected to control Georgia and neighboring South Carolina with such a small force? The British field commander, Lieutenant Colonel Archibald Campbell (1739–1791), wrote of his "hope of my receiving a Reinforcement of 6000 Loyalists from the back countries in Conjunction with the Indian Tribes who were attached to Government." His commanding officer, Major General Augustine Prevost (1723–1786), explained that the "object" of the expedition "was to open the back country, to bring to the test the often made professions of loyalty of its inhabitants." But the Indians never appeared and the promised "6000 Loyalists" turned out to be a phantom force. Campbell was joined by 1,100 to 1,400 Tories, and their zeal disappointed. As Campbell put it, they "could not be much depended upon in a general Action."[13]

Success or failure of Britain's southern offensive would be decided in the Back Country, for there lived between two-thirds and three-quarters of the white population of South Carolina, which was the main theater of war in the South. To put it in numbers, of the 74,000 whites (there were 104,000 blacks, all but about 10 percent in the Low Country) in South Carolina in 1775, almost 49,000 lived in the Back Country, with a little over 25,000 in the Low Country. Lord Cornwallis, who took command of British forces in the South after Sir Henry Clinton returned to New York, put pen to paper on this issue: "The keeping possession of the Back Country is of the utmost importance. Indeed, the success of the war in the Southern District depends totally upon it." Sir Henry agreed, writing to Cornwallis, "I agree with you that success at Charles Town—unless followed in the Back Country—will be of little avail." He believed, however, that taking Charleston "in the advantageous manner we have done it, ensures the reduction of this [South Carolina] and the next province [North Carolina]." But then he qualified that by echoing the words of General Prevost that we quoted earlier: "if the temper of our friends in those districts [Back Country] is such as has always been represented to us." Thus the British high command in America always had nagging doubts about the rosy scenario of hordes of loyal subjects in the Back Country created by exiled royal governors and in America by, as a junior British officer wrote, "people of too sanguine Expectations."[14]

The officer was right. Colonel Robert Gray, a prominent Tory militia commander, estimated Tory strength in South Carolina at "about one third of the whole," although he did put the population of the far Back Country district of Ninety Six as half Tory. A careful modern student of the Tories in South Carolina placed their number "at about 22 percent."[15]

At this point we should discuss the white inhabitants of the Back Country. They were for the most part poor. They had chosen to enter a hard land, raw and crude, and they matched their environment. In the mid-Back Country settlers were in the Camden area in the 1730s. The first settlers in the far western Back Country probably arrived as early as 1740. They faced daunting prospects. Rarely if ever has Hollywood captured the stark reality of Back Country and frontier America. It was to the settlers a new-found land, demanding backbreaking labor to clear virgin forests and fields for farms. Few roads, and those poor excuses, many rivers and streams but no bridges, lonely cabins here and there, scattered settlements. Travel was a nightmare. The Anglican cleric Reverend Charles Woodmason described a journey to baptize several children as "A Shocking Passage. Obliged to cut the way thro' the Swamp for 4 miles, thro' canes and impenetrable Woods—had my Clothes torn to Pieces." Was Woodmason's journey for naught? A man who was born and grew up there recalled in his old age that religion "had been for several years neglected, as is usual in almost all new settled countries. For when people have to labor hard, live hard—and that on coarse food and wear ragged clothes—they have little to spare, and it is hardly worthwhile for preachers, lawyers, doctors or dancing masters to attend their case, until they get, at least, one suit of clothing and other things in proportion." These conditions would last for many decades well into nineteenth-century rural America, leading a woman in Kentucky to recall that there was much marriage between cousins because the roads were so bad young people didn't get to meet many people.[16]

The newcomers in the far Back Country settled "on the Cherokee path between the Little Saluda [River]" and the settlement of Ninety Six and survived by "hunting or farming." They were a hard, crude people. A "root, hog, or die" mentality prevailed in their struggle to survive. And they brought that mentality to war.[17]

The commander of Fort Moore, situated on a bluff on the South Carolina side of the Savannah River, some six miles below Augusta, Georgia, had a mixed opinion of them. He thought the men were better hunters than the Indians, and in 1751 he reported that the best way to fight Indians was to recruit the "White Hunters abt the Congarees and Salude . . . for they are in general very expert Woods men but might perhaps exceed their orders as they are little more than white Indians." This was a common opinion of the inhabitants of Back Country America among the gentry and those who fancied themselves gentry: "those back settlers or Rifle-men are a parcel of Riff-Raff" was heard in the South Carolina Assembly. Of the Scotch-Irish among them, the Reverend Woodmason wrote, "ignorant, mean, worthless, beggarly Irish Presbyterians, the Scum of the Earth, and Refuse of Mankind," although another opinion that boded ill for the invaders had it that "In the art of War they are well skilled, & when in action as bold and intrepid as the Ancient Romans." John Rutledge (1739–1800), wartime governor of South Carolina, referred to Back Country folk as a "pack of beggars." George Washington, who knew the Back Country settlers up close over many years, regarded them with a disdain he carried to his grave as "A Parcel of Barbarian's and an Uncooth Set of People." Another Founder, and the first Chief Justice of the United States, John Jay, wrote to Thomas Jefferson in 1786 that settling the frontier meant "white savages" replacing "tawny ones."[18]

The men who rode behind the Colonels to Musgrove's Mill were Jay's "white savages," Rutledge's "pack of beggars." The Rice

Kings of the Low Country started the rebellion against British rule in the Deep South. But it was the "white savages," the "pack of beggars," and their leaders who saved the Rice Kings' Revolution.

Before departing for New York on June 5, 1780, Sir Henry Clinton appointed his man, Major Patrick Ferguson (1744–1780), as Inspector of Militia to maintain control throughout South Carolina once the regulars moved on. Ferguson had come south with Sir Henry's expeditionary force that captured Charleston. He commanded provincial regulars, the 175-strong American Volunteers who were drawn from eight northern provincial units. Clinton described Ferguson as "a very zealous, active, and intelligent officer." He was certainly zealous and active, and intelligent except for the last act of his life. We should spend a bit of time on Ferguson, for he would play one of the leading roles before and following the Battle of Musgrove's Mill. An observer wrote of him, "a strange adventurer tho' a man of some genius." He has come down to us as a "humane" officer, as he was described in the *Oxford Dictionary of National Biography*. He was not. Ferguson wrote Sir Henry a series of letters, August 1778–March 1780, in which he advocated a scorched earth policy to put down the rebellion. Among a range of measures, he recommended unleashing the horrors of Indian wars throughout the country, and in the Connecticut River Valley marching up the west side to Springfield in southwest Massachusetts, burning Rebel "houses, grains and fodder," marching down the east side and doing the same, "& thus in a fortnight destroying the Granary of New England." This from a man who is reported to have stated, "We came not to make war on women and children, but to relieve their distress."[19]

Ferguson's assignment in the Carolinas was to raise "a body of militia to act offensively with the army" and "a domestick militia for the maintenance of peace and good order throughout the country." In other words, control the Back Country after most of the regulars moved on. Ferguson pursued his assignment with zeal and would be a key player in an event that had a profound effect on the outcome of the Revolutionary War—in which the Battle of Musgrove's Mill would play a significant role.[20]

But Ferguson's mission would be complicated by a Rebel militia already in place, well organized and seasoned, whereas Tory militia leaders would have to be selected and the rank and file raised, armed, and organized, a time-consuming process. Of the nine Rebel militia units that provided men for the Musgrove's Mill operation, three had been established in 1775, one in 1776, another in 1777. The Rebels had been in control for five years. British Major General Augustine Prevost recognized this. "It must be said for the back country people . . . that the Rebels were already in arms and in possession of all the passes so as to prevent in a great measure every chance of communicating with the King's troops, besides having considerable bodies in different parts of the country purposely watching their motions." Rebel militia had also gained operational experience in the Snow Campaign of 1775, which decisively defeated the Tory attempt at counterrevolution, and also the successful 1776 campaign against the Cherokee in Appalachia. And as historian Jim Piecuch has pointed out, the Tories had been weakened by the flight in March-April 1778 of many of the boldest Tories, some 600 from South Carolina and 200 from Georgia, to sanctuary in British East Florida. Some of these men may have joined Colonel Thomas "Burntfoot" Brown's East Florida Rangers, a unit Colonel Elijah Clarke came to know well, and others the South Carolina Royalists, a provincial unit he and his fellow colonels would face at Musgrove's Mill.[21]

Further complicating British efforts, Sir Henry appointed Ferguson Inspector of Militia without consulting Lord Cornwallis, who would command in the South once Sir Henry returned to New York. Nor did he inform him until afterward. Sir Henry then boarded ship for New York. Cornwallis was not pleased. In a letter of May 30, to Cornwallis about his appointment, Ferguson assumed that his Lordship had received a copy of his instructions. Cornwallis replied on June 2 that although he had been informed of Ferguson's appointment, he had not received the instructions. He further informed Ferguson that he was "busied in forming a plan" for the establishment of militia and when he completed it

"I will transmit it to you. In the meantime, I must desire that you will take no steps in this business without receiving directions from me."[22]

To declare that Cornwallis was leery of Ferguson and his abilities would be an understatement, and Cornwallis' man, Lieutenant Colonel Nisbet Balfour, made his feelings about Ferguson clear from the beginning. "As to Ferguson, his ideas are so wild and sanguine that I doubt [fear in eighteenth-century usage] it would be dangerous to entrust him with the conduct of any plan."[23]

Despite misgivings, by June 30, 1780, Cornwallis believed that the situation in the Back Country was under control. He wrote to Sir Henry that the "capitulation" of Ninety Six and the "dispersion of a party of rebels who had assembled at an iron-works on the northeast border of the province . . . put an end to all resistance in South Carolina." In the same letter, he expressed confidence "that with the forces at present under my command . . . I can leave South Carolina in security and march the beginning of September with a body of troops into the back part of North Carolina, with the greatest probability of reducing that province to its duty." This despite his knowledge that ten days before he wrote this rosy picture had suffered its first major crack.[24]

Ramsour's Mill (modern Lincolnton, North Carolina) is about twenty miles north of the South Carolina line, thirty-four miles northwest of Charlotte. To call the action there a battle would lend it a formality it did not possess. It was a clash of two armed mobs. And not an Englishman within sight or sound. But it was deadly nonetheless and had a significant impact on the southern campaign.

Cornwallis instructed North Carolina Tories to remain quiet "and by no means to think of rising" until he marched into their state in early September. But the Tories led by a native of the area, Lieutenant Colonel John Moore, reacted to movements by Rebels. Moore was an officer of a Tory militia regiment, the North Carolina Volunteers. He summoned fellow Tories to join him at Ramsour's Mill. By June 20, 1780, 1,300 Tories were on a ridge overlooking Ramsour's Mill, although at least a quarter were unarmed. Despite being heavily outnumbered, 400 Rebels attacked and turned the Tory flanks. The fighting was often hand to hand, men bashing in skulls with clubbed muskets. Dead men were found after the battle with gunlocks buried in their heads. The Tories fled the ridge.[25]

It was the second time North Carolina Tories had met overwhelming defeat. At the first action, Moore's Creek Bridge in 1776, in the southeastern corner of the state near the coast, Highland Scots loyal to the Crown suffered a stinging defeat and rout and were knocked out of the war for five years. With regard to Ramsour's Mill, that fine small unit combat commander and future governor of North Carolina William Richardson Davie (1756–1820) wrote, "in a few days that district of country lying between the [Catawba] River, the mountains" and the South Carolina line "was entirely cleared of the enemy."[26]

It is of more than passing interest to note that even if Ramsour's Mill had never occurred, Cornwallis could not, as he stated a few paragraphs above, have marched into North Carolina in early September "with the greatest probability of reducing that province to its duty." For he faced an invisible enemy, at that time the curse of the Deep South, that would devastate his army—malaria. He wrote to Clinton on August 23, 1780, the height of the sickly season that lasted from May to October. "Our sickness is great and truly alarming. The officers are particularly affected. Doctor Hayes and almost all of the hospital surgeons are laid up. Every person of my family [his staff] and every public officer [brigade majors, Quartermaster Department officers, and others] of the army is now incapable of doing his duty."[27]

Between Tarleton's crushing defeat of Buford on May 29, and the rout of Tories at Ramsour's Mill on June 20, there had been, by conservative count, five engagements of varying intensity in South Carolina between Rebel and Tory militia: Alexander's Old Field, Mobley's Meeting House, and Stallion's were Rebel victories; Colonel Thomas Brandon's Defeat a Tory militia victory; and the destruction of Hill's Iron Works by Captain Christian Huck

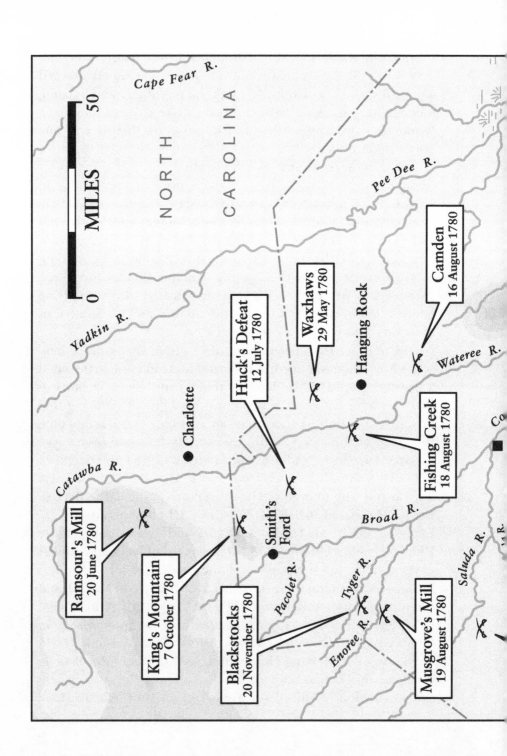

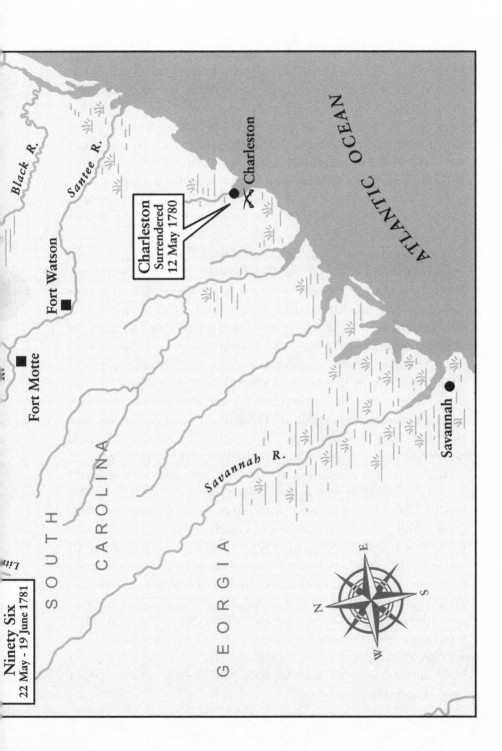

and a detachment of the British Legion a provincial victory. After Ramsour's Mill, and before the Battle of Musgrove's Mill, there were eighteen engagements, again of varying intensity, between the two Back Country enemies. At least twelve were won by the Rebels. The most notable was Huck's defeat on July 12, 1780. Rebel militia attacked an unsuspecting enemy at daybreak and not only defeated but killed Captain Huck, the destroyer of Billy Hill's Iron Works, and decimated his command of provincials and militia. It appeared that the partisan militia was not so overawed by the appearance of British and provincial regulars that they were ready to throw in the towel.[28]

Thus began a full blown and merciless civil war between Americans that is best expressed in German—Bruderkrieg (Brother's War). It raged for two and a half years, was dominated by the Rebels, and stymied the British pacification effort. A contemporary historian claimed that it left 1,400 widows and orphans in the Ninety Six District alone, and a participant wrote that the civil war "destroyed more property, and shed more American blood than the whole British army." In the Orangeburg District of the mid-Back Country, the famous Rebel militia commander General Thomas Sumter observed that "The Number and Retchedness of the Women & Children Cant be Conceived. Utterly out of the power of Many to Move or Subsist Much longer where they are."[29]

Who were these militiamen? These "beggars," who rebelled against the king of one of the most powerful countries in the world? These "white savages" who followed the Colonels to Musgrove's Mill? And where did they obtain the sinews of war, for militia had no commissary? James Potter Collins, who went to war at sixteen, tells us: "There was nothing furnished us from the public; we furnished our own clothes, composed of coarse materials. . . . We furnished our own horses, saddles, bridles, guns . . . and our own spurs; we got our powder and lead as we could, and often had to apply to the women . . . for their old pewter dishes and spoons, to supply the place of lead." They had "several good blacksmiths among us" and "we soon had a pretty good supply of swords and butcher knives."[30]

They were a fractious lot, the militia, civilian soldiers who brought to war their civilian ways of doing things. Colonel William Richardson Davie, who often led militia into battle, recalled that "in those times [it] was absolutely necessary" for officers to explain to their men what they proposed to do, and then the men would decide whether to accept their officers' plans and follow them. On one occasion later in the war, militia refused to serve under the officer sent to command them and demanded their own choice, for "they say they are Volunteers and shod be treated with distinction." About the same time, with a major battle looming, South Carolina and Georgia militia serving in northern North Carolina so resented their deployment during an action to provide covering fire for regulars that they decided to go home. They felt they had been improperly used and unnecessarily exposed to British fire. Consultation, persuasion, and agreement were absolute requirements, and we can be sure that is what happened when the Colonels chose men and explained to them their intention to lead them against the Tories at Musgrove's Mill.[31]

And then there was the matter of their beloved horses. Southern militia differed from northern militia only in that they were mounted soldiers in the finest cavalry country east of the Appalachian Mountains. During the Guilford Courthouse Campaign in February-March 1781, Major General Nathanael Greene needed more infantry before meeting Lord Cornwallis in battle. But when it was recommended that half of the mounted militia be dismounted to act as infantry, Greene met a stone wall of opposition. Desertion became rapid, and it was largely due to Greene's plan. In their defense, they were guerilla warriors, and in partisan warfare being mounted made them doubly effective against British troops and Tory provincials and militia attempting to bring them to action. If they were getting the worst of a firefight, or even holding their own but the time had come to depart the area, they mounted their horses and rode off. Later we will witness such an incident at the action at Cedar Spring that involved two of our Colonels. And the British did not have enough

regular cavalry in the South to challenge the Rebel partisans on
even terms. Lieutenant Colonel Francis, Lord Rawdon (1754–
1826), admitted that Rebel mobility was the reason why "we have
never been able to bring them to a decisive action."[32]

They were largely small Back Country farmers, most of whom
worked their fields without slave labor. An examination of the
pension applications of fifty-one men who fought at Musgrove's
Mill reveals that thirty-three joined Rebel forces in either 1775 or
1776 and served on and off until the end of the war. Those who
joined in 1775 had taken part in the so-called Snow Campaign—
called "Snow Camps" by participants—that defeated a Tory up-
rising against the rebellion. But unlike Continental regulars, they
did not sign up for the duration. Militiamen were part-time soldiers. They enlisted for set periods, ranging from two or three
months to longer or shorter times. Continental commanders
were driven mad when militia operating in conjunction with regular forces announced, even with a general action pending,
time's up, time to go home. (This practice would last into the
nineteenth century and bedevil General Andrew Jackson during
the Creek War of 1813–1814.) And in those cases nothing could
prevail upon them to stay. Also to be taken into account was the
livelihood of these men. There were spring plantings, crops to be
tended, harvests that would not wait. Early in the New York Campaign of 1776, during harvest season, George Washington alerted
the Orange County, New York, Committee of Safety, that at this
"extreeme busy season I cannot recommend your keeping the
Regiment embodied."[33]

Yet for all their fractious ways, had these "beggars" not risen
and bought the time necessary for operations by a refurbished
Continental Army under the brilliant Major General Nathanael
Greene, the Southern campaign, indeed the war itself, would
have taken on an entirely different hue.

In service militiamen were often safer. Decades later William
Kenedy, who fought at Musgrove's Mill, testified in his pension
application that after the British took Charleston in May 1780,
"The Tories commenced doing much mischief . . . in fact in that

country at that time it was dangerous for a Whig to remain at home, and they were of much more service to the country if they could act in a body." John Mills, who signed up in the Spring of 1776 at age fourteen, agreed in his application: "the disturbed state of the Country was such that it was considered more safe and desirable to be with the troops under arms than at home."[34]

But where did that leave the women and children? We quoted earlier Thomas Sumter's description of the wretched condition of women and children in the Orangeburg District in the mid-Back Country. Abarilla Wilbanks, widow of William Wilbanks, another Musgrove's Mill veteran, described her travail, and doubtless that of other women, when applying for her husband's pension: "he was absent a long time, she thinks five years . . . she made three crops without him; herself and her [three] little Boys; and had much trouble with the Tories during the absences of her husband . . . the Tories threw down her fences often & she had to put them up with her little Boys who were very young & small to do such labor, they also killed her hogs & Cattle and destroyed everything about the place, very often passing and committing all kinds of depredations." We can also safely assume that in areas of Rebel strength Tory women and children suffered similar treatment.[35]

Except for Abarilla Wilbanks, we have focused on men and will continue to do so, for this is mainly a book about fighting men. But unlike John Adams several years later we must not forget the women who were also active Rebels, kept children safe, the home fires burning, and saw as best they could to their men's welfare. Women kept their ears to the ground, obtained intelligence of planned or actual enemy movements, and in the case of Mrs. Jane Thomas rode sixty miles in the dark of night to warn her son and his comrades of an upcoming British attack. This led to a Rebel victory at the first battle of Cedar Spring. On other occasions women and children and old folks set up trestle tables in the woods and loaded them with hot food and drink to provide brief respites for Rebel bands. And Lieutenant Anthony Allaire of Patrick Ferguson's American Volunteers wrote of a Rebel village,

"This settlement is composed of the most violent Rebels I ever saw, particularly the young ladies."[36]

Following the action at Ramsour's Mill in North Carolina, there were by conservative count some 213 actions in South Carolina to the end of the war. The majority of these engagements were between Rebels and Tories, and the Rebels were victorious in most of them. This resulted in British officers early on losing faith in the Tory militia. Cornwallis found them "dastardly and pusillanimous." Nisbet Balfour believed that "The idea of militia being of consequence or use as a military force I own I have now totaly given up." And John Harris Cruger wrote to Cornwallis, "I think I shall never again look to the militia for the least support."[37]

They were right, and their feelings extended to the leaders of the Tory militia. The verdict on those men was delivered by one of their own, Tory Colonel Robert Gray, who declared that Rebel militia commanders "established a decided superiority in the militia line," whereas "The officers of the Royal militia being possessed themselves nor were able to inspire their followers with the confidence necessary for soldiers."[38]

In the weeks and months after the fall of Charleston in May 1780, the big three Rebel militia commanders who came to the fore were, in the Low Country, Francis Marion (1732–1795), a legend into our time as the Swamp Fox; in the mid-Back Country Thomas Sumter (1734–1832), uncooperative with Continental generals, yet Cornwallis wrote, "He certainly has been our greatest plague in this country"; and in the far Back Country the worthy Andrew Pickens (1739–1817), who took parole for five months after the surrender of Charleston but rejoined the fray in December 1780. Pickens' service was exemplary and his cooperation with Continental commanders tight. There were, however, other renowned and once famous Rebel militia commanders, among the finest the three Colonels of our tale.[39]

The operation against Musgrove's Mill came about when Colonel Charles McDowell of North Carolina established a camp at Cherokee Ford on the Broad River, later changing his location to about 8.4 miles downstream to Smith's Ford. As described later in the narrative, he was eventually joined by Colonels Clarke, Shelby, and Williams and probably some 300 to 500 partisans and several other Rebel officers. Their purpose was to foil Major Patrick Ferguson's efforts to bring the Back Country under the control of the invader. According to one of our primary sources, Major Samuel Hammond, the officers "consulted" with Colonel McDowell "on the propriety of making an excursion into South Carolina, to look at the enemy, and to commence operations against their out-posts, if they should be found assailable with our force." McDowell sent two "active and enterprising men" to scout for what we call today targets of opportunity. They reported back that there were 200 Tory militia forty miles south at Musgrove's Mill on the Enoree River.[40]

What was at Musgrove's Mill besides 200 Tory militia? Edward Musgrove had probably established his mill at a ford on the Enoree River in the early 1760s. There are several fords up and down the Enoree, but the site of the mill was where the road that served the western Back Country crossed the ford. Edward Musgrove ground corn and wheat grown by area farmers. He had made clear to Rebel leaders at the outset of the rebellion that he was neutral, and he remained neutral throughout the war and continued to turn grain into flour.[41]

There is no evidence that the mill or the land around it was fortified, participants in the battle did not mention it, and I do not believe that there was any type of fortification. There may have been a hospital on the site for Loyalist wounded. As described in the next chapter, after the early August clashes between Rebel militia and Ferguson's force, Tory wounded were sent to Musgrove's Mill to be attended by a Dr. Ross (probably William Ross). The word *hospital* should not be misconstrued. The wounded in this war were lucky if they had the shelter of a tent. As a Rebel put it, "I had seen the hospitals in Philadelphia, Princeton, and Newark, and would prefer dying in the open air of the woods." Probably militia were kept at Musgrove's Mill to keep communications open with the British post of Ninety Six, about thirty-two miles to the south. But it is hard to believe that they would have been able to maintain 200 militia at Musgrove's Mill for an extended period. As we shall see, one militia regiment was there for another purpose.[42]

Meanwhile, back at Smith's Ford plans were being laid that led to the Battle of Musgrove's Mill—a battle that would never have taken place had the Rebels known of a calamity suffered by an American army three days before.

We must ask ourselves, why was an American regular army needed in the South? After all, the southern Back Country militia had halted in its tracks the British pacification effort. The hitch was, despite the failure of the Tory militia to control the Back Country and British pacification stymied, the Rebel militia could not drive the British army from the South. That awaited a regular American army, the Continentals, waging war in cahoots with the militia. For the time being, the war in the South was also stalemated.

To replace the army lost at Charleston, a second American army marched southward under the temporary command of a European volunteer, Major General Jean, Baron de Kalb. The army probably would have fared far better had de Kalb remained in command. Alas, Congress chose its darling, Major General Horatio Gates, to command in the Southern Theater. Gates was a man of modest abilities, though he thought otherwise. It is true that in overall command at the Battle of Saratoga in October 1777, directing from afar, Gates won the greatest American victory of the war. At Saratoga in northern New York State, Gates forced the surrender of Lieutenant General John Burgoyne and his army of about 5,000 British and German regulars. Gates gauged his opponent well, waged a defensive battle, and had under him several fine combat commanders who led the troops in fierce fighting in the field. In his history of the Saratoga Campaign, Kevin J. Weddle rightly states that Gates "deserves to be remembered as the victor of Saratoga." Gates assumed command of the Southern army on July 25, 1780. In less than a month, he would lead that army to disaster.[43]

In mid-August 1780, at Charles McDowell's camp at Smith's Ford on the Broad River, Colonels Clarke, Shelby, and Williams were probably in the final stage of choosing men and horses for the raid on Musgrove's Mill. On August 16, 1780, at Camden, South Carolina, where two armies faced each other, Gates was 200 yards behind the front lines, unlike Cornwallis, who was up close so he could see what was happening when the armies clashed and if necessary ride to a crisis—which his Lordship did during the battle. Gates commanded 3,052 Continentals and militia, the latter from eastern North Carolina and Virginia. Cornwallis led 2,239 troops, most of them regulars. At Camden Gates proved his incompetence at and lack of stomach for combat command. His army was routed, the survivors following the Hero of Saratoga in his 180-mile flight northward on the fastest horse in the army to Hillsborough, North Carolina.[44]

For the time being, however, we can set aside Gates' calamity, which had a sharp effect on a decision made by the Rebels at Musgrove's Mill, and meet our three Colonels and follow them to their rendezvous.

*TWO*

# The Colonels

## COLONEL ELIJAH CLARKE

Elijah Clarke (1742–1799) was an illiterate frontiersman.[1] The Georgia Tory Elizabeth Lichtenstein Johnston had men like Clarke in mind when she wrote that in the American Revolution "the scum rose to the top." He is unknown today, even in his adopted state of Georgia, yet he was one of the leading southern militia commanders. Elijah Clarke could always be found up front, leading his men into battle—"Agile, Mobile, and Hostile."[2] He was wounded so many times his body must have been a mass of scars. His reputation as a fierce battlefield fighter was attested to by one of his fellow Colonels at Musgrove's Mill. A friend of Colonel Isaac Shelby wrote, "It was in the severest part of the action that Colonel Shelby's attention was arrested by the heroic conduct of Colonel Clarke. He often mentioned the circumstances of ceasing in the midst of battle to look with astonishment and admiration at Clarke fighting." In Chapter 1 we quoted Cornwallis labeling Thomas Sumter as his "greatest plague." After the Battle of Blackstock's, mistaken in believing that both Sumter and Clarke had been killed, Cornwallis paid a similar tribute to Clarke. "We have lost two great plagues in Sumpter and Clarke."[3]

To British officers and the American gentry, men like Clarke were crackers, described by a British officer as "that *heathen race* known by the name of *crackers.*" In 1772 the acting governor of Georgia, James Habersham, wrote to Governor James Wright, who was in England, "The present intruders I am informed are persons who have no settled habitation and live by hunting and plundering the industrious settlers. You will easily distinguish" that the "people I refer to are really what you and I understand by Crackers." It is a word meaning braggart brought from the mother country that can be found in Shakespeare's *King John,* act 2, scene 1: "What cracker is this same that deafs our ears With thus abundance of superfluous breath?" The word is still in active use in America, synonymous with rednecks, trailer trash, and other terms of contempt. It is worthy of note that Eric Adams, the current black mayor of New York City, was forced to apologize when the media revealed that in 2019 he called white cops "crackers." Elijah Clarke was a cracker and he led crackers.[4]

In 1780 a pro-British newspaper printed an unflattering but accurate description of the men who followed Elijah Clarke: "Clarke's party is said to have consisted of men, whose restless dispositions, or whose crimes prevented their living in any country where even the resemblance of government was maintained, and therefore taking themselves to the vacant lands on the frontiers; living without any control; they made frequent inroads upon the industrious inhabitants of the back settlements, and have frequently involved the Province in wars with the Indians."[5] Clarke's band included a Chowanoac Indian, who may have been a mixed blood, Indian and black; and a slave, Austin Dabney, who was given his freedom after fighting under Clarke.[6]

Born in Anson County, North Carolina, as an adult Clarke was apparently one of the first white settlers in the South Carolina

Back Country, at Grindal's Shoals on the Pacelot River. In 1773, two years before the Revolutionary War began far to the north on Lexington Common, with his wife Hannah and their children Clarke moved to the frontier of Georgia on what was called the Ceded Lands, later Wilkes County.

Clarke became a Rebel against British rule and by 1776 was a captain of militia. He was wounded that year while leading a wagon train that was attacked by Cherokee warriors. It was the first of many wounds he would suffer during the war. He led militia the following year against Creek raiding parties. He was promoted to Lieutenant Colonel and took part in Georgia's third and final badly organized attempt to take British East Florida. Some twenty miles inside Florida, always leading from the front, Clarke was shot in the thigh, almost captured, and carried from the field during an attempt to take Alligator Bridge, which crossed Alligator Creek, a tributary of the Nassau River just north of present-day Jacksonville. At that fight Clarke faced for the first but not the last time a Georgia Tory, Lieutenant Colonel Thomas "Burntfoot" Brown, commanding the East Florida Rangers (later the King's Carolina Rangers). The British commander in chief in the South at the time, Major General Augustine Prevost, described Brown as "a Young man entirely unacquainted with Military matters tho' otherwise Zealous and deserving." Three years later an American commander would write similarly of Clarke.[7]

Upon his recovery, Clarke was elected Lieutenant Colonel and second in command, under Colonel John Dooly (1740–1780), of the Wilkes County militia battalion on the Georgia frontier. At the time it was also known as the Ceded Lands, acquired in 1773 from the Creeks and Cherokees by the Treaty of Augusta as a result of Indian indebtedness to English traders. The Ceded Lands consisted of 2,100,000 acres, one cession a narrow strip near the coast, the other a much larger cession farther inland, between the Savannah and Ogeechee Rivers and twenty-two miles north of Augusta. Our interest, and Elijah Clarke's, centers on the large inland cession. Keep the Ceded Lands in mind, for they will come up again as our story progresses.[8]

We related earlier that in late December 1778 the British invaded Georgia, took Savannah, and with about 1,000 British and provincial regulars and militia marched 128 miles westward and occupied Augusta. A Tory militia force of 600 South and North Carolinians under Colonel John or James Boyd had entered the Ceded Lands with the aim of joining the British army in Augusta. But on February 14, 1779, at Kettle Creek, some 60 miles northwest of Augusta, the Tories were attacked and soundly defeated and Boyd killed by a 450-man Rebel band commanded by Colonel Andrew Pickens of South Carolina. Elijah Clarke and Colonel Dooly served under Pickens in this fight, described by Dooly as "at least 3 [h]ours Constant firing." Clarke had his horse "Shot Down" from under him. Despite his heroics in battle, according to Andrew Pickens, Elijah Clarke at the time lacked experience and discipline. Clarke and Dooly got bogged down in the swamps, and Pickens described their lateness in coming to grips with the enemy as not pressing "as I wished them. . . . This was not for want of courage but for want of experience and the necessity of obeying orders."[9]

Following the fall of Charleston and the British advance into the Back Country, Clarke seems to have first come to their attention in early August 1780. Lieutenant Colonel John Harris Cruger (1738–1807) wrote from Ninety Six that "in the neighborhood of the Ceded Lands in Georgia, a Colonel Clark (rebel) is very busey stirring the people up. I am told he has 300 men with him." A little over a week before Cruger mentioned him, Clarke and his men were in South Carolina riding with other Rebel forces. From Thicketty Fort, about twelve miles east of modern Spartanburg, South Carolina, Tories raided Rebels in the surrounding countryside. If we accept the memory of seventy-three-year-old Ebenezer Fain when he applied for a pension in 1836, action at Thicketty Fort was prompted by seventeen-year-old Ebenezer, an Over Mountain militiaman who had "joined Colonel Charles McDowell's Regiment." When "on sentry [duty] I shot a spy by the name of John Franklin and found an express from Lord Cornwallis to Captain [Patrick] Moore urging him to defend his fort and promising to reinforce him. We made a forced march to said fort at a place called Thicketty." Colonel Isaac Shelby, in command of a 600-man militia force, including Clarke and his Georgians, besieged Thicketty Fort. Captain Moore, commander of a garrison of ninety-four men, read the numbers and on July 30, 1780, surrendered without a shot being fired by either side.[10]

Clarke and Shelby teamed up again on August 8, 1780, at the southern edge of Spartanburg, either at a place once called Cedar Spring or a mile or so away at Thompson's Peach Orchard. The location is of small moment. Major Patrick Ferguson was in personal command of a combined force of militia and provincial regulars that received intelligence of a Rebel band collecting at Ford's Mills and gave pursuit on August 6. Lieutenant Anthony Allaire wrote in his diary, "We made a forced [night] march of sixteen miles in order to surprise them," but when they arrived the Rebels had already moved on another seven miles, The Rebel band, about 600 strong, consisted of Georgians led by Colonel Clarke and North Carolina Over Mountain Men commanded by Colonel Shelby. On August 7, Ferguson's column "Got in motion at seven in the evening and made another forced march on them," but the Rebels had mounted and decamped a half hour before Ferguson's advance arrived "at four o'clock on Tuesday morning, August 8th." The Rebels were three miles ahead at Cedar Spring. They knew that Ferguson, with between 400 and 600, was in pursuit and closing. Instead of fleeing, the Rebels deployed for battle.[11]

Major Ferguson reported to Cornwallis, "As our men and horses were totally overcome by two successive nights' marches . . . I therefore contented myself with detaching our mounted infantry . . . with the least fatagued of the militia horse." The British advance force of 144 dragoons and mounted militia were commanded by Captain James Dunlop, a provincial officer who had served in the Queen's Rangers and Dunlop's Corps but was now with Ferguson's American Volunteers. It was the first time Clarke and Dunlop (sometimes spelled Dunlap) would meet in battle. The following year their second encounter would lead to an atrocity. Ferguson and his main force were a few miles behind Dunlop. Allaire wrote that "Dunlap and his party rushed into the centre of the Rebel camp where they lay in ambush, before he was aware of their presence." The fighting was hand to hand, short and savage. Clarke, in the thick of it, was wounded by saber strokes to the head and neck but fought on. Dunlop was "slightly wounded." Between twenty and thirty of the British force were killed or wounded. But the Rebels could not risk an encounter with Ferguson's main force, once again mounted their beloved horses, and withdrew. Shelby wrote that the pursuit was continued for "several miles . . . on one of the warmest days ever felt." Allaire reported that "We pursued them five miles to the Iron Works but were not able to overtake them, they being all mounted." Lyman Draper claimed that when Ferguson and his troops gave up the chase but were still in view, Clarke and Shelby formed their men on a ridge and "bantered and ridiculed them to their hearts' content." If true, it would not be surprising if the Rebels mooned them.[12]

There is an interesting side note to this encounter. Both Lieutenant Allaire and Dr. Johnson reported that, to quote Allaire, "Sent the wounded to Musgrove's Mills, Enoree River to be attended by Dr. Ross."[13]

Eleven days later Clarke and Shelby would once again ride together into a fight—at Musgrove's Mill.

COLONEL ISAAC SHELBY
Isaac Shelby (1750–1826), in his time one of the most admired men in America, is unrecognized today. He was the son of a well-known frontiersman. Evan Shelby was born in Wales and at age sixteen was brought to America by his parents. His son Isaac was born in Frederick County, Maryland. Isaac received what he called "the rudiments of a plain English education," and as he grew older steeped himself, in his words, "in the art and cultivation of the land."[14]

In 1773 the family moved to southwestern Virginia, in what is now East Tennessee, and built a fort and trading post in the Holston River Valley near the present-day twin cities of Bristol, Virginia, and Bristol, Tennessee. Daniel Boone is said to have had an account at the Shelby trading post. It was a prime location on the path taken first by long hunters like Boone and later by tens of thousands of settlers on their way to the "Dark and Bloody Ground" called Kentucky.

The last Indian war before the War of the American Revolution was Lord Dunmore's War, October–November 1774, fought on the Virginia frontier against the Shawnee and Mingoes under the famous Shawnee leader Cornstalk. Contrary to the accounts of some historians, the war was not precipitated by white encroachment on Indian lands but by Indian raids against white farms and settlements on land that had been legally obtained from the Indians by treaty. The decisive and hard-fought battle of the war was waged at Point Pleasant, near modern Point Pleasant, West Virginia, in the Ohio River Valley. At the critical moment on October 10, 1774, with other officers either dead or wounded, Captain Evan Shelby "assumed command of the entire line of battle." His son Isaac served in the battle as a lieutenant of militia and acquitted himself well. Isaac Shelby sent a stark description of the fighting to his family. "We had a Very hard day its really Impossible for me to express or you to Conceive Acclamations that we were under, sometimes, the Hidious Cries of the Enemy and the groans of your wound[ed] men lying around was Enough to Shuder the stoutest hart."[15]

For Isaac Shelby, Indian fighting continued. In March 1775 the settlers on the Watauga and Nolichucky Rivers bought from the Cherokee their leased land. The following month, however, in far away Massachusetts, the shot was fired heard 'round the world. The War of the American Revolution had begun, and that changed the situation on the Southern frontier. The Cherokee, knowing well that the British were their only hope to stop land-hungry whites from invading their country, by the spring of 1776 sided with the Crown, demanded that the settlers vacate their land, and gave them forty days to comply. The settlers cinched their belts and stood their ground.[16]

The Crown's southern Indian agents asked the Cherokee to await a British offensive before attacking the settlements, but they also supplied them with 5,000 pounds of powder and lead and the Cherokee refused to delay their attack. War parties wreaked havoc east of the mountains, where "they spread desolation" and "Plantations lie desolate, and hopeful crops are going to ruin." Our concern, however, is with the lonely settlements on the western side of the Appalachians in what was then North Carolina and is now East Tennessee. Three columns totaling 600 to 700 warriors moved northward in the Great Valley and attacked the Watauga, Nolichucky, and Holston settlements. Isaac Shelby fought as a volunteer private in what Tennessee historians call the Battle of Island Flats. In reality, it was a relatively short fight, really a skirmish, but important as the frontiersmen denied the Cherokee their goal of wiping out the settlements.[17]

A breakaway faction of the Cherokee under Dragging Canoe moved southward and settled across the Tennessee River on Chickamauga Creek, thus the name given to them by the whites. In 1779, Isaac's father Evan led an expedition against the Chickamauga that was meant to end their raiding. It was temporarily successful, but it did not destroy the Chickamauga's military ability. They would remain inveterate enemies of frontier whites until their massive defeat in September 1794 by a Tennessee militia force under Major James Orr. Evan Shelby's expedition is of interest to us because his son Isaac revealed that he not only was a rank-and-file fighter and leader of men in battle but also displayed his knowledge and appreciation of the vital military specialty of logistics. Isaac Shelby was credited with supplying the army with transportation and supplies.[18]

Kentucky was Isaac Shelby's siren song. He was twenty-five when he ventured deep into Kentucky, spent the tough winter of 1775 alone, thirty miles from the famous fort of Boonesborough, and laid claim to 1,400 acres. He also claimed land for his father. Most Kentucky settlers of those early days lost their land because they neglected to keep careful records and file them with the proper authorities. But Isaac Shelby's meticulous records, filed first with the Transylvania Land Company and later with the Virginia Land Office, meant that he retained the lands he claimed for himself and his family.

When Shelby returned to the Holston River Valley he was a captain of Virginia militia. In 1777 he was appointed commissary by Governor Patrick Henry of Virginia. In that capacity he was responsible for supplying Continental forces as well as militia and frontier forts. Two years later he served in a force sent against the Chickamauga.

Meanwhile, the British, facing stalemate in the North, had turned southward. We covered the British invasion of the South and the activities of Major Patrick Ferguson in Chapter 1. Colonel Isaac Shelby first entered the war east of the mountains in mid-1780. By then Ferguson's efforts to subdue the South Carolina Back Country alarmed Rebels in North Carolina. Were they next?

Colonel Charles McDowell (1743–1815) commanded militia in Burke County, North Carolina, east of the mountains, and may have exercised regional command. In any case, he called upon Shelby to join him. Shelby mustered 200 mounted riflemen and set out. The Over Mountain Men who followed him lived on the cutting edge of the frontier, on land contested by the owners, the Cherokee, so whenever men rode east to join their countrymen to fight the British others had to stay behind to guard against attacks by Cherokee warriors engaged in trying to drive the invaders out. These fierce fighters were their own commissary. In his pension application of 1833, eighty-one-year-old Pharaoh Cobb testified that "this applicant found his own horse, gun, ammunition etc. While under Shelby we generally got our provisions from the Tories," which meant they plundered, as did both sides in this Back Country guerilla war. A British officer referred to the Over Mountain Men as "that cursed nest beyond the mountains."[19]

Less than a week after joining Colonel McDowell at Cherokee Ford on the Broad River and discussing the situation in South Carolina, Shelby headed for Thicketty Fort with 600 men. With him were Elijah Clarke and his Georgians. We covered the surrender of Thicketty Fort and subsequently Isaac Shelby's participation in the fierce action at Cedar Spring in the previous discussion of Elijah Clarke's activities. It is now time to take a look at the third colonel who would join Clarke and Shelby in the strike against Musgrove's Mill.

COLONEL JAMES WILLIAMS

James Williams (1740–1780), also unknown today, was the victim of a scurrilous campaign of calumny that blackened his name for almost two centuries. He was born in Hanover County, Virginia, and later moved with his family to North Carolina. Sometime after 1773 Williams and his wife settled in South Carolina's Ninety Six District, in the Little River area between the Broad and Saluda Rivers. There he became a farmer, miller, merchant, and big landowner. He was also one of the few Back Country settlers who owned slaves. A deeply religious man, in 1761 he may have been one of the founders of the Little River Presbyterian Church.[20]

There is no known image of Williams. He was described as "five feet, nine inches tall, and corpulent. His complexion was dark, his hair and eyes were black. He had a large nose with nostrils so large when distended," that one of his militiamen joked, "the boys had been hunting and had treed a possum in the Colonel's nose."[21]

Williams' standing in his community is revealed in 1775 by his election to South Carolina's First Provincial Congress and his appointment to the committee to execute the Association, a document produced by the Provincial Congress that required the signatures of citizens to support the rebellion. In other words, you were either for us or against us. In November of that year Captain James Williams also raised a company of militia. From late November 1775 to September 1779, he served in at least eight major campaigns and battles, including the July-October 1776 Cherokee expedition and the failed Franco-American siege of Savannah in September-October 1779. By either then or 1780 Williams was a colonel and commanded the militia regiment in the northeastern Ninety Six District.

Following the British invasion of South Carolina in late 1779 and the fall of Charleston early the following summer, and with it the surrender of the only regular American army in the Southern Theater, South Carolina Back Country Tories, who had been quiet since their defeat in 1775, became active. One Rebel they had their eyes on was James Williams. According to the Tory

David Fanning, Williams had a close call. As recounted by Fanning in his postwar narrative, sometime in early June he and William Cunningham decided "to take Col. Williams of the Rebel militia prisoner . . . Col. Williams got notice of it and pushed off and though we got Sight of him he escaped us."[22]

By June 10 Williams' plantation was occupied by Tory militia. But he had foreseen the British advance into the Back Country and Tory activities and had moved personal property and most of his slaves to his brother's farm in Caswell County, North Carolina. In his last will and testament prepared in Caswell County, Williams described himself as a resident of the Ninety Six District but "now a refugee in North Carolina."[23]

The British invasion and their establishment of strongpoints throughout South Carolina and at Augusta in adjoining Georgia caused the leading Rebel militia commanders in the Back Country to seek parole from the British and retire from the field. One of them, Colonel Andrew Pickens, would return to the fray about five months following the fall of Charleston after his "house was plundered of moveable property, and the remainder wantonly destroyed" by a British-Tory force. For the time being, however, a vacuum existed, and there appeared to fill it Thomas Sumter. Andrew Pickens gave us the measure of the man: "he was self important, and not communicative, I had little connection with him during the war." Williams had the misfortune to run afoul of South Carolina's prima donna.[24]

Sumter established a camp in North Carolina at Tuckasegee Ford on the east bank of the Catawba River, nine miles west of Charlotte. On June 18, 1780, militia leaders gathered there and elected Thomas Sumter their leader. Williams was in Sumter's camp by early July. The two men did not get along, a situation well known to South Carolina's governor in exile, John Rutledge (1739–1800), and to Lord Cornwallis. Rutledge reported that "Col. James Williams whose affair with Innes . . . was truly brilliant . . . is gone on with a Determination to distinguish himself as a Partisan, & I believe he will—I have put both him & Sumter (each of whom may be of service but they will never agree) under Genl.

Smallwood's Command." Cornwallis was equally well informed. He wrote Patrick Ferguson that "Sumpter has had a quarrel with Williams over command and has gone to Hillsborough to refer it to Gates."[25]

Will Graves has pointed out that Rebels in Sumter's camp came from different areas of the South Carolina Back Country, and their primary interests were to protect their home areas from British and Tory attacks. Sumter and his followers were from the "more central and upper part of the Back Country." Williams and the men who followed him were from the western area around the British post of Ninety Six, where enemy patrols were active. Captain Joseph McJunkin, who knew both men, reported the same difference. "About this time Col James Williams joined Sumter—the latter having a disposition to go Southward, and the former towards the West. Disagreeing in their notions, the troops joined with Sumter or Williams just as their own inclinations led them."[26]

In early August, probably a few days after the Battle of Hanging Rock on August 6, Colonel Williams with other militia officers from western South Carolina and followers left Sumter's camp and rode to Colonel Charles McDowell's camp at Smith's Ford on the Broad River. There Williams found Elijah Clarke and Isaac Shelby and joined them in choosing men and horses for the Musgrove's Mill operation.

Figure 1. Sir Henry Clinton, commander in chief of British forces in America, triumphed when his army captured Charleston, South Carolina, and the only American army in the South. He then returned to headquarters in New York City, leaving in command Lord Cornwallis, who was astounded when he learned of Musgrove's Mill. (*National Army Museum*)

Figure 2. Colonel Elijah Clarke, an illiterate frontiersman whose ferocity in battle at Musgrove's Mill caused one of his fellow colonels to stop in the midst of combat and stare in awe at Clarke fighting. (*Hargrett Rare Book and Manuscript Library, University of Georgia Libraries*)

Figure 3. Colonel Isaac Shelby went from rifleman in the ranks to one of the most important Rebel commanders of the war and a planner and participant in both the Battle of Musgrove's Mill and the game-changing Rebel victory at King's Mountain. He is shown here much later in life. There is no known image of the third Colonel, James Williams. (*New York Public Library*)

Figure 4. Charles Cornwallis, upon hearing of the defeat at Musgrove's Mill, thought it "impossible that there can be any enemy openly in arms near the frontier after the total rout of Gates and Sumter." (*New York Public Library*)

Figure 5. Banastre Tarleton. His victory over a Continental regiment in Wax-haws and what Rebels believed was an ensuing massacre helped lead to a rising against the British and hundreds of actions that included the consequential Rebel victory at Musgrove's Mill. (*New York Public Library*)

Figure 6. The battleground at Musgrove's Mill today reveals as it did in 1780 the clear field of fire provided the Rebels under cover on the ridge as Tory provincials and militia marched into a mini-Bunker Hill. (*John Foxe*)

Figure 7. Patrick Ferguson. He reaped the consequence of Musgrove's Mill when he led his command of over 1,000 to disaster and his death at King's Mountain.

Figure 8. The death of Patrick Ferguson at King's Mountains. The Battle of Musgrove's Mill led directly to the Battle of King's Mountain, the turning point of the Revolutionary War in the South. (*Anne S. K. Brown Military Collection, Brown University Library*)

*THREE*

# "Dead Men Lay Thick on the Ground"

Two HUNDRED "picked men well mounted" led by Colonels Clarke, Shelby, and Williams rode out of Colonel Charles McDowell's camp at Smith's Ford on the Broad River "one hour before sundown" on August 18, 1780, and pushed hard for Musgrove's Mill. They had forty miles to go. Communications being what they were in those days, dependent on couriers on horse and foot—in the words of one scholar, "time consuming beyond current imagination"—they did not know of Gates' disaster two days before at Camden. Nor did the British know of them. Lord Cornwallis and his officers believed that after Camden there was "no other enemy embody'd" except Thomas Sumter's militia force. Neither the British nor the Colonels knew that Sumter and his band had been routed at Fishing Creek on the Catawba River by Banastre Tarleton and his British Legion on the same day that the Rebels began their ride to Musgrove's Mill.[1]

Take a moment and consider these men. They were seasoned fighters from three states—North Carolina, South Carolina, and Georgia. The North Carolina contingent from both west and east of the mountains was commanded overall by Colonel Isaac Shelby. The Washington County Regiment of Over Mountain Men had fought in eleven actions, including Island Flats, the Chickamauga expedition, the Cherokee expedition, and the hand-to-hand fighting at Cedar Spring. The other Over Mountain unit was the Sullivan County Regiment, also well blooded. A Tory, Drury Mathis, would later see the Over Mountain Men in action at King's Mountain and never forgot them. Mathis lay badly wounded on the slope. He "used to relate that as the mountaineers passed over him he would play possum; but he could plainly observe their faces and eyes; and to him those bold, brave riflemen appeared like so many devils from the infernal regions, so full of excitement were they as they darted like enraged lions up the mountain. He said they were the most powerful looking men he ever beheld; not over-burdened with fat, but tall, rawboned and sinewy, with long-matted hair—such men, as a body, as were never before seen in the Carolinas."[2]

The Back Country partisans were also fierce fighters. East of the mountains the Burke County Regiment was commanded by Major Joseph McDowell, brother of Colonel Charles McDowell. Burke County men had served in fourteen actions and had been at the major fight at Ramsour's Mill.

In Chapter 1 we quoted a British officer who described the Back Country men "as little more than white Indians." From the 1776 expeditionary force against the Cherokee to Cedar Spring in 1780, in between long hours in the saddle on scouting missions, they had proven themselves. Joseph Hughes had joined up at fourteen, marched with the men who in 1776 invaded Cherokee country before he rode behind the Colonels to Musgrove's Mill. William Kenedy had ridden to Charleston in 1776 to fight the British at the Battle of Sullivan's Island and after Musgrove's Mill would serve at two legendary battles that changed the course of the war—King's Mountain and Cowpens. John Mills also joined in 1776 at fourteen and became a veteran fighting with the Cherokee expedition. Alexander Peden first saw action in the 1775 "Snow Camps" Campaign. We could go on. Suffice it to say that every man among them was accustomed to war and rough life in the field.[3]

South Carolina was represented by five militia regiments, in overall command of Colonel James Williams. The Little River District Militia, formed in 1775, had twenty-seven fights under its belt before Musgrove's Mill. It was commanded by one of our primary sources, Major Samuel Hammond. A detachment from the 1st Spartan Regiment, also raised in 1775, was blooded in fourteen actions. The 2nd Spartan Regiment, mustered in 1775, had served in sixteen actions. The South Carolina units were rounded out with the Lower (Dutch Fork) District Company of Militia, and Roebuck's Battalion of Spartan Regiment of militia that had been raised in 1780 following the British invasion. Musgrove's Mill would be Roebuck's first action as a unit.

Colonel Elijah Clarke's militia detachment from Wilkes County had first seen action on the Georgia frontier against the Cherokee and had followed Clarke to South Carolina for the fights with Ferguson's provincials and militia.

The Over Mountain Men were famed as expert riflemen. And there were certainly riflemen among the Back Country militia. Recall the insult delivered at them earlier by a member of the South Carolina Assembly: "those back settlers or Rifle-men are a parcel of Riff-Raff." Some probably carried muskets, faster loading than rifles but only accurate up to about eighty yards, whereas rifles were deadly far beyond that range. Other Back Country militia may have been armed with various types of guns, perhaps including fowling pieces loaded with shot.

Consider also the darkness they rode through. To capture the full flavor of that eventful night almost 250 years ago, we must try to imagine darkness we never know, a world whose nights were filled with almost constant dark, not the half dark to which we are accustomed but a Stygian gloom between sundown and sunup, relieved if the weather was right only by the moon and the stars. The difference between that night in 1780 and our time can also be measured in silence as well as darkness. People made noises, and so did animals and the wind and rain and other sounds of nature, but there were no motors, no constant hum of traffic in the distance. There was a stillness both day and night that is rarely found outside of the great empty places.[4]

Through that darkness and stillness rode men with a purpose, men who knew fear in the face of danger but pushed on with grace under pressure. "Picked men well mounted."

They did not know the actual whereabouts of Major Patrick Ferguson's some 1,000 Tory militia and about 70 to 100 provincial regulars. Nor do we know the specific route the Rebels took. Two of our primary sources locate Ferguson nearby. According to Colonel Shelby, they thought Ferguson with his entire force was "only two or three miles" from their line of travel. Captain Joseph McJunkin recalled that after the battle "Col. Ferguson whom we had just passed a little on our right, must also have heard our firing, & not knowing but that they would break in on us . . . and serve us worse than we did the Tories." Had Ferguson been located where they thought, it spoke to their fierce resolve to complete their mission despite the risks of either being intercepted or leaving a far superior enemy force behind them. But Ferguson was nowhere near the Rebels.[5]

Ferguson had been camped about a week earlier overnight at Josiah Culbertson's plantation on Fair Forest Creek, which was in the general area the Rebels were riding through. On August 11 he began moving in a southeasterly direction and by the night of the 17th he was bivouacked as the crow flies forty-six miles southeast of Musgrove's Mill at the plantation of the Rebel militia officer Colonel Richard Winn (near modern-day Winnsboro, SC). But the Rebel band did not know that, and some thirty-four years later Colonel Shelby wrote that to evade Ferguson, "They traveled through the woods until dark, then took the road, and traveled fast all night great part of the way in a canter, never stopped even to let their horses drink." Another rider, Major Samuel Hammond, claimed that they "halted and fed and refreshed for an hour." Whatever the details of their ride, they had rivers and creeks to ford, for there were no bridges in the Back Country: Gilky's and Thicketty, Pacelot and Fair Forest, and finally the Tyger. The Rebels reined-in on a timbered ridge a mile and a half north of the Enoree River ford at Musgrove's Mill "just at break of day." There a surprise awaited them.[6]

Colonel Shelby reported that a man who lived nearby appeared and said "that the enemy had been strongly reinforced." Musgrove's Mill was no longer manned by only 200 Tory militia. The night before 150 provincial regulars had arrived. They were from the British post at Ninety Six, as the crow flies thirty-two miles to the south.[7]

The newcomers were commanded by a Scot, Colonel Alexander Innes (pronounced Inn-es) (1743–?). Innes was well regarded by his superiors. In January 1777 General Sir William Howe, then commander in chief of British forces in America, appointed Innes Inspector General of Provincial Forces. Innes started the office of Inspector General and ran it for the rest of the war. He would later become a favorite of Cornwallis and Balfour. Although Innes was in New York at the time, he was appointed commander of the South Carolina Royalists when the regiment was formed in St. Augustine in May 1778. The Royalists were comprised of Tory refugees from South Carolina who had fled to British East Florida. On December 29, 1778, Innes was with the British assault force commanded by Major Archibald Campbell that went ashore at daybreak and by sundown conquered Savannah. Some two weeks later he met his command when the South Carolina Royalists arrived in Savannah. But he and the Royalists had only about a week to take each other's measure before Innes boarded ship for London. We may reasonably speculate that Innes behaved well during the assault on Savannah, for he was given the honor of carrying Major Campbell's dispatches informing the government of the victory at Savannah. Innes was either in England or returning when the South Carolina Royalists, about 320 strong under Lieutenant Colonel Joseph Robinson, marched to Charleston as part of a force of 1,500. Innes arrived in time to take part in the siege. He served east of the Cooper River under Lord Cornwallis, assigned by his Lordship "to keep a good look-out" for either reinforcements for the Rebel garrison in Charleston or if the garrison tried to break out. Following the fall of Charleston, he was stationed for a while in New York City. Innes was described by a New York Tory who knew him "as a man, whose haughty and supercilious conduct has estranged more minds from His Majesty and the British Govt than perhaps all the other blunders in the conduct of this American War put together."[8]

Colonel Innes' "conduct" extended to his opinion on the situation in South Carolina, which he expressed to Cornwallis in early June, almost two and a half months before Musgrove's Mill. From Friday's Ferry on the Broad River in the mid-Back Country, he wrote that the Loyalists "are assembling in many places, and the most violent rebels are candid enough to allow the game is up and are coming in to make their submission in great numbers." Moreover, "I can assure your Lordship there will not be a shadow of opposition in the province attempted, and I speak from the best authority." He then assured Cornwallis, "I will pledge my life that three hundred men shall march to the Indian line [about thirty-five miles west of Ninety Six] and from thence to Augusta without firing a shot."[9]

Innes' deputy, Major Thomas Fraser (1756–1820), a fellow Scot, was a merchant in Virginia when the war began and served as an officer under the royal governor, Lord Dunmore. After the Revolutionary War began, Fraser was a lieutenant in the Queen's American Rangers and later a captain in the New York Volunteers. Under Innes, he was field commander of the South Carolina Royalists and served in that capacity during the rest of the war. Balfour described Fraser as "extremly intelligent and active." Fraser's post-war history is interesting. He was placed on the Provincial half-pay list, but instead of exile in Canada or elsewhere in the Empire, he retired to South Carolina, married a local woman, owned sawmills on the Edisto River, was in the lumber business, and later entered into business in Charleston. He collected half pay until his death, and the Crown gave his widow a pension.[10]

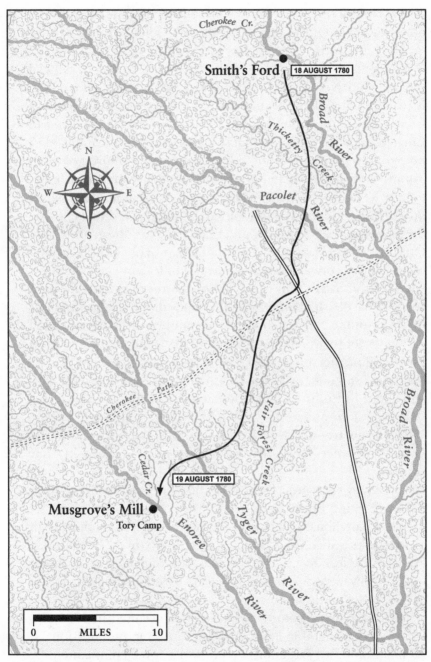

The movements of the three Colonels, August 1780. While the locations of Smith's Ford and Musgrove's Mill are known, the exact route is speculative.

Fifty of the regulars were Colonel Innes' mounted South Carolina Royalists. Of the fifty who followed Colonel Innes to Musgrove's Mill, thirty-five were new recruits.

Lieutenant Colonel John Harris Cruger, a sterling provincial officer from New York City who had taken command of the British post at Ninety Six after Balfour was made commandant of Charleston, did not think well of the Royalists. He reported to Cornwallis in early August "that the South Carolina Royalist[s] in point of discipline are quite militia and not an hundred of them arm'd." In a book written after the war, a British officer, Lieutenant Roderick McKenzie, described the regiment as "lately raised, and indifferently disciplined," though he did claim that the Royalists "behaved with great gallantry" at Musgrove's Mill. On July 28 Innes wrote to Cornwallis that "The South Carolina regiment in its present state is really not fit for any active service." Yet after the battle Innes claimed of the recruits that "no men cou'd behave with greater spirit than they did in the late affair of the 19th ultimo." So much for the certainty of primary sources.[11]

The other provincial regulars were first rate: about fifty from 1st Battalion, DeLancey's Brigade (Lieutenant Colonel Cruger's battalion) of New Yorkers, Captain George Kerr commanding; and about fifty of the Light Company, 3rd Battalion, New Jersey Volunteers, commanded by Captain Peter Campbell (1756–1822). From Trenton, New Jersey, Campbell had served with the Volunteers since December 1776. He died in exile in New Brunswick.[12]

DeLancey's Brigade was raised in New York in September 1776, following the British invasion the previous June. The 1st and 2nd Battalions took part in the capture of Savannah in 1778 as well as the successful defense of that city in 1779 against a Franco-American force. The 2nd Battalion remained at Savannah until the city was evacuated in July 1782. The 1st Battalion arrived at Ninety Six in the summer of 1780.[13]

The New Jersey Volunteers were also recruited in 1776 and had seen considerable action in the North. On one mission 1st Battalion and 3rd Battalion served in the force commanded by

Major Patrick Ferguson in his surprise attack and defeat of Pu-
laski's Legion at Egg Harbor, New Jersey, an action notable for
the free use of the bayonet. The 1st and 3rd Battalions also served
in the capture of Savannah and its later successful defense. The
3rd Battalion arrived at Ninety Six shortly before the Battle of
Musgrove's Mill.[14]

The Tory militia that would take part in the ensuing action was
the 100-strong Dutch Fork Regiment commanded by Colonel
Daniel Clary (1710–1795). McDowell's spies had accurately reported the number of Tory militia at 200. But the 100-man Ninety
Six District Brigade of Loyalist Militia was not at Musgrove's Mill
that day. It had been sent on patrol before the Rebels arrived to
Cedar Ford, eight to nine miles east of Musgrove's. Lieutenant
Colonel Cruger wrote on August 4, "For Ferguson's support I
have order'd Clary's regiment of militia to be immediately assembled and to receive his orders." On August 9, Clary was reported
to have marched for Ferguson's camp. It appears that his march
was delayed in order to join Innes' command. Still vigorous at
age seventy, Clary and wife Eleanor Deveron Clary (1715–1761)
had at least eleven children and perhaps fourteen. Clary was a
popular man in his district. After the war, although fined and
barred from political activity, he remained in South Carolina. The
famous Tory Captain David Fanning, who had been scouting
along the Indian lines, with fourteen militiamen joined Innes at
Musgrove's.[15]

Colonel Innes and his regulars were not at Musgrove's Mill to
reinforce the militia. He had been ordered by Lord Cornwallis
on August 13, to march from Ninety Six and reinforce Major
Patrick Ferguson and his militia and provincials. Innes arrived at
Musgrove's Mill on the evening of the 18th. He intended to de-
part on the 19th, the day the Rebels under Clarke, Shelby,
Williams, and their 200 riders arrived at the ridge overlooking
the ford on the Enoree. Writing on August 19, Ferguson expected
Innes to arrive that day at Lisles Ford (or Lyles) on the Broad
River about one mile upriver from where the Enoree joins the
Broad, "and will, I imagine, advance tomorrow after us." Pure co-

incidence had brought the Rebels and Innes' command to within a mile and a half of each other.[16]

The 200 Rebels did not know that the Tory militia across the Enoree Ford had been reduced by about 100 and no doubt thought they faced some 350–400 of the enemy. But they were still outnumbered, now opposed by 250 and not just militia but also provincial regulars. Yet they could not call off the operation and depart the area. There is no evidence that they planned to hunker down, avoid detection while resting, and then ride off. Their horses were blown from the torrid pace set during the night and their riders fared little better. Colonel Shelby recalled that they "were too much broke down to retreat" and "prepared for battle as fast as possible." Their horses were picketed under the guard of sixteen men about three hundred yards behind the ridge. The fighting force on the ridge was now reduced to 184 men.[17]

Two mounted scouts were sent out to reconnoiter. They crossed the Enoree, discovered the enemy force, and were returning when they ran into a Tory patrol. Shots were exchanged. Shelby is the only primary source that mentions Tory casualties during the exchange of fire. The Tory patrol reported back that Rebels were in the area while the Rebel scouts rode to the timbered ridge to report their findings to the Colonels.[18]

Upon hearing the crackle of firearms and receiving the report of the Tory patrol, Colonel Innes and his officers met in the Musgrove home for a so-called council of war. This was reported years later by descendants of Edward Musgrove. They said the family overheard the Loyalist officers discussing the situation. According to Musgrove family tradition, the junior officers advised that before acting they await the return of the 100 militia riders who had been sent out that morning on a patrol to Cedar Ford. The Musgrove family claimed that Colonel Innes overruled his officers and ordered them to form the troops and prepare to cross the Enoree and engage the enemy.[19]

The Battle of Musgrove's Mill has been described as an ambush, a word often used loosely. Even David Fanning, a participant, misused the word. It was not an ambush. In an ambush, one side is totally surprised by a hidden enemy. One might argue that the Tories were surprised by the appearance of Rebel scouts, yet they had their own patrol out plus the 100-man patrol to Cedar Ford, evidence that they felt the necessity of continually being on guard. And would Colonel Innes have ordered out his entire command and crossed the river unless he suspected, perhaps knew, that a large Rebel force was on the other side of the Enoree? Lacking such knowledge, the wise course would have been to send a strong mounted patrol to scout across the river. And it is well within the realm of possibility that, as the Colonels were warned by a local man of the presence of provincial regulars, another local may have alerted Innes to the arrival of a Rebel band across the Enoree. Whatever he knew, Innes mustered his entire force.[20]

The Rebel line on the timbered ridge a mile and a half from the ford stretched some 300 yards. There is no evidence from participants that the line was semicircular, as is often claimed. In front of the Rebels was an old "Indian field" that had been planted and burned over for generations and provided a clear field of fire. There was no overall commander on the ridge. According to Major Hammond, the three Colonels "agreed" that the command "should be conjoint." I therefore believe we can safely assume that the Colonels had a brief discussion on tactics and quickly agreed what to do. There is no evidence of wrangling or disagreements. Colonel Shelby and his North Carolina Over Mountain Men were stationed on the right (west), Colonel Williams with his South Carolinians in the center, Colonel Clarke and his Georgians on the left (east). In his report dated September 5, 1780, seventeen days after the battle, Colonel Williams wrote that "Twenty horse were ordered on each flank, waiting the Enemy's Approach." He also reported that he ordered "every man take his Tree." Colonel Shelby, however, claimed that they made "a breastwork of logs and brush which they completed in half an hour." Shelby is the only source that mentions a breastwork. Philemon Waters, a grandson of Edward Musgrove, stated that the day after the action, "at least a hundred men, women and children" visited the battlefield, "and yet not one ever said anything afterwards of a brush breastwork thrown up (by the Americans)." (It should be noted that the purpose of the visit by some civilians the next day was repeated on many a Back Country battlefield—to discover if their loved ones were among the corpses and wounded scattered across the killing field.) I believe the Rebels took to trees in open order.[21]

The Colonels and their men awaited the enemy's appearance. They had not long to wait. Colonel Innes with his provincials and militia forded the Enoree and advanced in three columns, provincials in the middle, militia on their flanks. Major Hammond reported that they came on "in full trot." As was the custom then, their officers, regular and militia, were on horseback. The Rebel Captain Shadrack Inman and "sixteen well mounted, expert riflemen" had been dispatched by the Colonels to "Scrimmage with the enemy as soon as they crossed the river" and "draw them on to attack us on the hill." According to Major Hammond, upon withdrawing these sixteen men were to remain mounted and fire upon the enemy from their left flank while another sixteen riders did the same on the enemy's right flank. These two groups were probably what Colonel Williams meant when he reported "twenty horse . . . on each flank," either he or Hammond mistaking the numbers involved. Let us leave it at sixteen or twenty riders on each flank. The Rebel force on the ridge now numbered 144–152, facing 250 of the enemy advancing on them.[22]

One wonders if the effort by the group led by Captain Inman was necessary. By crossing the river, Colonel Innes had signaled his goal of attacking the Rebels on the ridge. High on the ridge at the main line of resistance the waiting Rebels would have heard, faintly at first, increasingly louder, the drums of the regulars. Steadily, drums beating, the regulars and militia advanced on the ridge. At 200 yards, the provincials were ordered to deploy from column into "line of battle" and continued to advance. At 150 yards from the waiting Rebels the provincials were halted and ordered to prepare to fire. Colonel Williams reported that "then began a very heavy fire," which suggests that there may have been more than one volley.[23]

Whatever the case, firing at 150 yards was useless. Their muskets were only accurate up to about eighty yards. If the firing was meant to frighten or disperse the Rebels, it failed. On the ridge, the Colonels and their men waited for the enemy to get closer. After firing, the Loyalist regulars would have been ordered to advance up the hill at trail arms. Almost certainly bayonets were fixed. Cold steel would win the day.[24]

Here a question is in order. Neither Colonel Innes nor Major Fraser had been at Bunker Hill in Boston in 1775, where British regulars suffered staggering casualties before prevailing when the New England militia ran out of ammunition. Thereafter, that experience tempered British tactics in the North when confronting Rebel militia behind cover. But surely Innes and Fraser had heard about it, especially Innes when he served in New York and would have had the opportunity to speak to officers who had been at Bunker Hill. The man who appointed him Inspector General of Militia, Sir William Howe, had commanded at Bunker Hill. And Lord Rawdon, Cornwallis' deputy in the field, whom both officers knew, had been at Bunker Hill, where he behaved with gallantry. So we must ask—why did Innes send his regulars forward in standard battle formation against a foe under cover? Did it stem from his "haughty" personality? . . . We do not have an answer.

As the regulars advanced, the only Rebel fire was delivered by the mounted flanking parties. The Rebels on the ridge waited for the order to fire. At what range was the order given? Depending on which source you accept, they fired at forty, fifty, seventy, or eighty yards. Williams reported that the men were ordered not to fire until "the Enemy came within Point blank Shot . . . and not fire until the order was given." That order, Hammond stated, would be a "single shot from Colonel Shelby," whereupon the men were "to be steady and take good aim." Although Hammond first gave the distance as fifty yards, in his next paragraph he states that the signal to fire was given at forty yards. Whichever distance is correct, both were well within Rebel killing range.[25]

The first Rebel volley staggered the enemy: "their ranks were thinned," Hammond reported. They fell back a short distance. But the provincials—at least the 100 from New York and New Jersey—were well-disciplined, seasoned troops. Their officers rallied them, they reformed, and again surged forward. Colonel Shelby recalled that they got "within a few yards of our works." No primary source supports Lyman Draper's oft-repeated story that Shelby's "right flank of his right wing gradually" gave way and that Clarke "sent his small reserve to his aid, which proved a most timely relief." I do not believe it happened.[26]

The second Rebel volley was devastating. Colonel Innes and Major Fraser were seriously wounded, unhorsed, and carried from the field. Every provincial officer except two were wounded. All of the three New Jersey Volunteer officers were wounded. Stripped of most of their officers, the regulars fell back in disorder, and the Tory militia ran for their lives. An officer of the South Carolina Royalists, Lieutenant Colonel Evan McLaurin, probably was not at Musgrove's Mill, perhaps at nearby Ninety Six. But he certainly talked to participants shortly after the battle. McLaurin reported that "The militia at that time behaved as usual. The greatest part fled and left a few honest men to be sacrificed. The necessity of not depending on the Militia will daily become more evident." Innes described the militia's behavior as "dastardly and cowardly."[27]

The Rebels then left their trees and charged into the fleeing enemy. It was at this point that Captain Abraham De Peyster heard the chilling sounds he would later refer to at King's Mountain as the "damned yelling boys." They were the war cries of Shelby's Over Mountain Men resounding over the battlefield. Major Hammond has the Rebels rushing "on with more boldness than prudence," and "the mounted riflemen on both flanks charged into the ranks of the retreating foe." Colonel Shelby wrote that "the slaughter from thence to the Enoree . . . was very great," observing, "dead men lay thick on the Ground over which our men pursued the enemy." Shelby continued: "This action was one of the hardest ever fought in the United States with small

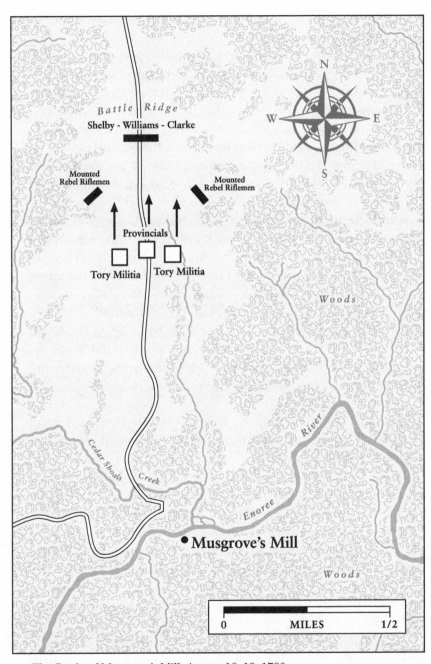

The Battle of Musgrove's Mill, August 18–19, 1780.

arms. The smoke was so thick as to hide a man at the distance of twenty yards."[28]

There is a Lyman Draper story about the Tory militia officer Colonel Daniel Clary that may be true and in any case is too good to ignore. In the confusion of the pursuit, two Rebels grabbed the "opposite bits of his horse's bridle," whereupon with great presence of mind, Clary shouted, "Damn you, don't you know your own officers," and "He was instantly released, and fled at full speed." I repeat the tale because some of Clary's descendants still live in the area, some of them have passed down the story, and I decided that family tradition should be honored.[29]

The Rebels pursued the broken Tories. Colonel Williams wrote, "we drove them about Two Miles." This would have taken them across the Enoree. No source mentions the Rebels crossing the river. David Fanning recalled that the Tories "Retreated about a mile and a quarter where we encamped." Both men were probably mistaken about the distance. I accept Hammond's account, which states that the enemy "re-crossed the river in great disorder. On our part, we were so scattered and out of order, that it was determined to halt, form, and send for our horses to cross the river."[30]

Once the Tories were on the other side of the Enoree, one of the regulars' two unwounded officers, Captain George Kerr of DeLancey's Brigade, was able to reestablish order and form a rear guard. The fighting was over.

How long did the actual fighting last? When the Rebels were ordered to fire, Colonel Williams reported that "A warm fire began that lasted about 15 minutes." Colonel Shelby recalled that "The action was bloody and obstinate for upwards of an hour and a half." I believe it would be reasonable to assume that Williams was more or less right about how long the Rebel fire lasted at the main line of resistance, and that Shelby was more or less right if he meant the initial action plus the pursuit and fighting for a mile and a half to the Enoree ford.[31]

The Battle of Musgrove's Mill was a mini-Bunker Hill. At the famous Battle of Bunker Hill in Boston in 1775, the British fielded 2,000 to 2,500 officers and men, depending on which source you accept. Of these, all credible sources agree that the British suffered 1,054 killed and wounded. If we accept the high figure of British afield, their casualties were just shy of 50 percent. That figure included 89 officers—19 dead, 70 wounded. One historian wrote, "Of all the British officers who would fall in battle in the eight years of the Revolution, nearly one-quarter did so at Bunker Hill."[32]

The Loyalist toll at the little known Battle of Musgrove's Mill was similar, with only two of the seven provincial officers present unwounded. Colonel Williams, in his official report to Major General Horatio Gates written only seventeen days after the battle, reported Rebel casualties as "Three Killed on the field, Eight Wounded, one of which is Mortal." (One of the Rebel dead was Captain Shadrack Inman.) The Loyalists, however, suffered grave losses. Colonel Williams claimed sixty dead, "the greatest part British." (Rebels referred to provincials as British.) In his pension application, Edward Doyle claimed that "I saw fifty-two dead bodies on the field of the Enemy—and among them a British captain." The testimony of Colonel Williams and Doyle gives added weight to the charge that the Tory militia broke quickly, ran fast, ran far. And it is reasonable to speculate that the Rebels concentrated most of their fire on their formidable foe—the provincials. Doyle added, "it was said Col. Innis was wounded in the neck," which was true and adds credibility to his account. If we accept Colonel Williams' account of sixty dead, Innes lost 40 percent of his force before we count the wounded. Unfortunately, Williams gave no count of enemy wounded, but he did claim seventy prisoners taken. In fact, no Rebel primary source extant even gives a number for enemy wounded, nor is there a credible secondary source for the wounded. We do, however, have two British sources, and I am indebted to Mark Stanford, Interpretive Ranger at the Musgrove Mill Historic Site, for bringing them to my attention. John Harris Cruger wrote to Cornwallis on August 21 and with his letter sent "A return of the killed, wounded, and missing." Unfortunately, that letter and the return are not extant. Cornwallis, however, in a letter of August 23 to Clinton reported, "I have since a report that Lt. Col. Innes fell in on the 19th with a party of rebels, when he was deserted by the militia, and himself wounded in the neck, and about fifty officers and men of his Provincials killed, wounded, or taken." That information probably came from Cruger's missing letter and return of August 21, and we may surmise that Cruger was referring only to Innes' regulars. Using the figures provided by Williams, Doyle, and Cornwallis, I believe the provincial killed and wounded ranged between fifty and sixty men. I accept Williams' claim of seventy prisoners taken as it was he who took the prisoners to Hillsborough, North Carolina. If we count Loyalist casualties as sixty killed and wounded and seventy prisoners, Innes suffered casualties of 52 percent.[33]

Yes, the Battle of Musgrove's Mill was indeed a mini-Bunker Hill. And in tandem with the famous battle, it goes far in revealing the brutal nature of the Revolutionary War.

The Rebels were elated. Deep in strong Tory country they had routed provincial regulars. Lord Cornwallis, astounded upon receiving news of Innes' defeat, still unaware of the passions aroused in the Back Country by the British invasion, wrote to Colonel Cruger, "I am very anxious to hear of Colonel Innes, having been told that he is wounded." He then expressed not just astonishment but disbelief that a Rebel force was in arms in the Back Country. "It is impossible that there can be any enemy openly in arms near the frontier after the total rout of Gates and Sumter."[34]

The Colonels meanwhile decided to augment their victory by pushing on and taking the important British post of Ninety Six, described by Colonel Shelby as "weak and defenseless." As they were about to set off, however, a courier arrived from Colonel McDowell and handed over a letter McDowell had received from Major General Richard Caswell (1729–1789), who had commanded the North Carolina militia at the Battle of Camden. His letter informed McDowell of General Gates' calamity. The Colonels had no choice. Behind them a victorious British army and, they still thought, Patrick Ferguson and his large militia force stiffened by the American Volunteers. As McKeen Greene, a nineteen-year-old militiaman serving under Colonel Clarke, put it years later in his pension application, "we must fly for our lives." The attack on Ninety Six was called off. The Rebels turned their horses northward.[35]

Even if Camden had never occurred, the Rebels were fortunate not to have attacked Ninety Six. Shelby was wrong. Ninety Six was a strong, fortified post commanded by an outstanding provincial officer from New York City, Lieutenant Colonel John Harris Cruger. He would prove his ability the following year during Nathanael Greene's failed siege of Ninety Six. Later that year, at the Battle of Eutaw Springs, one of the hardest fought and bloodiest battles of the war, Cruger received a signal honor. Instead of following the usual practice of assigning battlefield commands to British officers, the British commander, Lieutenant Colonel Alexander Stewart, gave Cruger command of the main line of resistance. After the battle, Stewart praised Cruger for his "conduct and gallantry during that action."[36]

Meanwhile, forty-six miles away, Major Patrick Ferguson had been ordered on August 18 to move against the Rebel militia leader Thomas Sumter, whom the British believed was the only unit "of what the Rebels can call a Corps in these parts at present." As we know, Sumter had been routed by Banastre Tarleton and his British Legion on that same day. But Lord Cornwallis in Camden did not yet know that. On August 19, the day of the battle, Ferguson was preparing to pursue Sumter "with Vigour." Dr. Uzal Johnson, a surgeon with Ferguson's militia, wrote that preparations began in the early evening to move out in pursuit of Sumter, and at seven o'clock "we got in motion." At that very moment, however, an "express arrived from Coll. Innes" informing Ferguson of the battle and wounds suffered by him and several other officers. He "must immediately have assistance as many of the militia had left him." Four hours later Ferguson's command of some 1,000 men moved out for an all-night "rapid march that way," wrote Ferguson's adjutant, Captain Alexander Chesney.[37]

While this was going on the victorious Rebels, with their seventy prisoners in tow, were pushing hard for North Carolina. They had to be exhausted after their long nighttime ride followed by a ferocious battle. Major Joseph McJunkin recalled that "We got our water as we passed the brooks, & hunger was so great that we pulled green corn and ate it as we marched," and Colonel Shelby noted that "they made use of peaches and green corn for their support." To spare their horses, they probably dismounted occasionally and trotted alongside. Colonel Shelby also wrote that Ferguson's Tories were in pursuit and followed for "fifty or sixty miles, until their horses broke down and could follow no further." He stated that when they reached safety in North Carolina, "The excessive fateague to which they were subjected for two nights and two days effectually broke down every officer . . . that their faces & eyes swelled and became bloated in appearance as scarcely to be able to see."[38]

Referring to General Gates' disaster at Camden, Shelby also recalled that "This action happened at the most gloomy period of the Revolution, just after the defeat and dispersion of the American army." It was certainly a gloomy period in the South, but no gloomier than after the calamitous defeat of the main American army on Long Island in 1776 and the loss of New York City; or the gloom felt by many in 1777 after Washington's defeats in Pennsylvania at Brandywine and Germantown, which led to efforts by intriguers to reduce the Great Virginian to just another general subject to a board of war. But Shelby was not alone in recalling gloom at this time in the Carolinas. Major Hammond remembered "a general depression of that period." Yet referring to the victory at Musgrove's Mill, first calling it a "clear speck on the horizon, which would have been otherwise very much overcast," he wrote, "This little affair, trifling as it may seem, did much good . . . our numbers continued to increase from that time, and all seemed to have more confidence in themselves." Remember Major Hammond's words.[39]

# FOUR

# "This Little Affair, Trifling as It May Seem"

WE MUST NOW ADDRESS the significance of the Battle of Musgrove's Mill. It is claimed that Elijah Clarke's failed siege of Augusta and his flight with followers and their families seeking refuge beyond the mountains "had an immediate and tangible impact on the wider war in that it led directly to the October 7, 1780 Battle of King's Mountain, the turning point of the Revolution in the South." The evidence given for this is in a letter from Lord Cornwallis to Sir Henry Clinton about "poor Major Ferguson" written about two months to the day after King's Mountain.

> He obtained my permission to make an incursion into Tryon
> County whilst the sickness of my army prevented my moving.
> As he had only militia and the small remains of his own corps
> without baggage or artillery, and as he promised to come back
> if he heard of any superior force, I thought he could do no
> harm and might help keep alive the spirits of our friends in
> North Carolina, which might be damped by the slowness of

our motions. The event proved unfortunate without any fault
of Major Ferguson. A numerous and unexpected enemy came
from the mountains. As they had good horses, their movements were rapid. Major Ferguson was tempted to stay near
the mountains longer than he intended in hopes of cutting
off Colonel Clarke on his return from Georgia. He was not
aware that the enemy was so near him, and in endeavouring
to execute my orders of passing the Catawbaw and joining me
at Charlottetown, he was attacked by a very superior force and
totally defeated on King's Mountain.[1]

On the contrary, Ferguson had every intention of staying near
the mountains. He not only knew where the enemy was, as we
shall see he challenged them. His Lordship's explanation is dis-
sembling. The fault was entirely Ferguson's. And he was not attacked by a "very superior force." Ferguson's command at King's
Mountain slightly outnumbered the Rebel army of Back Country
partisans and Over Mountain Men.

After Musgrove's Mill, Clarke returned to Georgia and in September besieged Augusta, a tale that will be told in the Epilogue.
The siege failed four days after it began and Clarke and his followers fled for the mountains with the enemy in pursuit. What
concerns us at this point is that John Harris Cruger wrote to Cornwallis, "If they escape us . . . I am in hopes Ferguson may cross
upon them. I have given him notice." Ferguson did try to inter-
cept Clarke and believed on September 28, "it is probable that
we shall cross upon him this evening or tomorrow." But on October 1, "I have in vain looked for Clark, who I believe has escaped
by a difficult pass at the head of Saluda." Supporting evidence for
Ferguson's quest is in the entry of September 30 in Lieutenant
Allaire's *Diary*. "Lay at James Step's with the expectation of inter-
cepting Colonel Clarke . . . but he was prudent enough to take
another route." And in his *Journal* Dr. Uzal Johnson recorded on
September 28, "having intelligence that Coll. Clerk [Clarke] was
coming this way from Georgia. A Guard . . . were left . . . to keep
a good lookout." But by October 1, "no certain intelligence of
Clerk [Clarke]." As the crow flies, James Step's was about thirty-

six miles south of modern Asheville, North Carolina, in the foothills of the Blue Ridge Mountains.[2]

Major Patrick Ferguson, however, had another reason to venture deeper into North Carolina that was at least equally, and I believe far more, important to him than his search for Clarke. Well before the action at Musgrove's Mill, at least sometime in June 1780, Ferguson had pleaded for permission to invade North Carolina. On June 27, Lieutenant Colonel Nisbet Balfour, then commanding at Ninety Six, reported to Cornwallis that "Ferguson and his militia at Sugar Creek have great matters in view and I find it impossible to trust him out of my sight. He seems to me to want to carry the war into North Carolina himself at once." On July 3 Cornwallis replied, "*Entre nous,* I am afraid of his going to the frontier of North Carolina and playing us some cussed trick." How prophetic of his Lordship. Sometime between August 22 and September 1, after the August 19 Battle of Musgrove's Mill, Ferguson met with Cornwallis in Camden, during which Cornwallis explained to Ferguson "what part I intend that the militia should take in my future operations. I will then speak to you about your corps and every other business that I have not time to take notice of in this letter." At that meeting Cornwallis gave Ferguson permission to march into the North Carolina Back Country, nestling against the eastern side of the Blue Ridge Mountains, which are the eastern and southeastern range of the Appalachians.[3]

Ferguson's pursuit of the Rebel victors at Musgrove's Mill had failed when his men's horses broke down. But Major Patrick Ferguson was not a man to ignore his aim to bring those Rebels and others to bay and punish them. In fact, on August 19, the day Musgrove's Mill was fought but before Ferguson knew of it, he wrote in revealing language to Cornwallis' aide-de-camp, Captain Alexander Ross. "I shall consider it as the spirit altho not the letter of his Lordship's orders to strike at them." The letter makes clear that he is referring to the Rebel band that rendezvoused at Charles McDowell's camp on the Broad River, from which the "picked men well mounted" were recruited for the raid on Musgrove's Mill, and he named among others McDowell and Clarke. And as we shall see, there can be no doubt that he also meant that "cursed nest" of mountaineers moving back and forth between North and South Carolina.[4]

Shortly after Musgrove's Mill, Isaac Shelby and other Rebel leaders were planning to deal with Ferguson. It was at this "gloomy period of the Revolution," Shelby wrote, "that Colonel Shelby, Colonel [John] Sevier, Colonel [William] Campbell and General [Charles] McDowell who had fled to their country began to concert a plan for collecting a force & making a forced march to surprise Major Ferguson with his party who had advanced up to the foot of the Mountains on the East side and threatened to cross over and lay waste the Country on that side for their opposition to his Majesties' arms." A courier service was established to keep everyone informed of Ferguson's movements. Captain David Vance of the North Carolina militia called them "newsbearers." James Jack and Archibald Nail were assigned to bear news "over the yellow mountain to Shelby," Joseph Dobson and James McKay to Benjamin Cleveland and Herndon, Robert Cleveland and Gideon Lewis from Benjamin Cleveland to Shelby. "Thus the news went the rounds as fast as horses could carry their riders."[5]

Ferguson's threat against the Over Mountain Men, as expressed by Shelby in the previous paragraph, was real. He sent a Rebel prisoner, Samuel Phillips, a distant kinsman of Isaac Shelby, over the mountains with a famous verbal message: "If they did not cease and desist from their opposition to the British arms, he would march over the mountains, hang their leaders, and lay their country waste with fire and sword."[6]

The Overmountain Men and their leaders needed no further goad. On September 26, 1780, reinforced by riflemen from adjoining Virginia, they set out for the lands east of the mountains where they rendezvoused with Carolina Back Country militia commanded by Colonel Benjamin Cleveland, all 300 pounds of him, and Major Joseph Winston. They were 910 strong when they caught up with Ferguson on October 7 on a ridge in South Carolina that rises sixty feet above the surrounding countryside and is called King's Mountain. Ferguson was about thirty miles from Charlotte and Cornwallis' army. He could easily have reached the safety of the army's lines. But he chose instead to stand and fight. Why?

Deserved or not, Ferguson had a reputation for being difficult. He was a Clinton protégé serving under Clinton's enemy. He did not belong to Lord Cornwallis' club of young favorites: Balfour, Rawdon, Ross, Tarleton. But a smashing victory would set things right. Odd man out but proud, ambitious, ardent warrior, he must have brooded on this, and in such temper judgment clouds, delusions gather, glory beckons. Banastre Tarleton spoke for the ages on the subject: "The more difficulty, the more glory."[7]

Ferguson's decision led to his death in battle and the destruction of his command of some 1,100 men—killed, wounded, captured. Because of the calamity, Cornwallis called off his invasion of North Carolina, retreated to South Carolina for the winter, and when he emerged in the spring he faced a new American commander of the southern American army, Major General Nathanael Greene (1742–1786), who had much to teach his Lordship about the art of war. The impact of Ferguson's disaster on the British cause was made clear by Sir Henry Clinton. In his postwar memoir, Sir Henry wrote that King's Mountain "unhappily proved the first link in a chain of evils that followed each other in regular succession until they at last ended in the total loss of America."[8]

Let us, therefore, be clear on the significance of the Battle of Musgrove's Mill. It was "this little affair, trifling as it may seem," that set the stage for that "first link in a chain of evils."

# Epilogue

## What Happened to the Colonels?

### COLONEL ELIJAH CLARKE

Clarke missed the pivotal battle of King's Mountain. He was otherwise engaged in Georgia. Returning to the Wilkes County frontier, he hoped to recruit over 1,000 men and capture Augusta, which was rich with supplies and British presents for the Indians. But he was only able to assemble about 430 militia. Some joined willingly, others were motivated by threats. John Harris Cruger later wrote to Cornwallis that "thirty odd have surrender'd themselves and arms to me . . . most of them poor wretches who were carried down by force and threats from Clark and his adherents." A Rebel, Joshua Burnett, testified in his pension claim that Clarke "sent word to those who had surrendered [prior to the action at Augusta], that if they did not meet him at a certain noted Spring in a wilderness . . . he would put every one of them to death." The problem of recruitment dealt with in Clarke's inimitable way, he headed for Augusta, which was held by the King's Carolina Rangers commanded by none other than Colonel Thomas

"Burntfoot" Brown, one of Clarke's Tory foes in 1778 at the Alligator Bridge fight in Florida. Brown was a member of the gentry,
the opposite of Clarke the rough-hewn frontiersman. But he was
just as tough as Clarke. Five years before, facing alone a gang of
Rebels in the Augusta he would now defend, Brown underwent
physical and moral terror that would have broken many a man.
His skull fractured by a clubbed rifle, his legs tarred, his feet held
over burning wood, two toes lost—thus the Rebel epithet—
scalped, paraded through town in a cart, he emerged from his
ordeal with a thirst for vengeance.[1]

Colonel Brown's occupation of Augusta, with responsibility for
maintaining order in the adjoining region, was part of wider
British policy to reestablish royal authority in the Southern Back
Country. Brown's force consisted of 180 rank and file led by seven
officers and twelve sergeants. Also with him were 100 convales-
cents of the New Jersey Volunteers and his own, 500 Indians, and
35 civilians of the Indian Department. A British officer described
Augusta as "a Number of straggling Houses, arranged in a long
Street lying parallel to the [Savannah] River," which flowed 100
yards from the town. His description belied Augusta's importance. As the great naturalist William Bartram observed, Augusta
"commands the trade and commerce of vast fruitful regions
above it, and from every side to a great distance," reflecting its
significance as an entrepot stretching westward into Indian country, and northward deep into South Carolina. Augusta was one of
the keys to the Back Country, and also to the Creek Indian frontier.[2]

On the morning of September 14, 1780, Clarke approached,
divided his command, and attacked from different directions.
Brown received word that the Indian camp three miles away had
been attacked and immediately marched to its relief. He suc-
ceeded but then found that the "enemy had entered town by a
back road" and "we returned instantly to give them battle." One
of Clarke's units had taken the Indian trading post made of stone,
known as the White House, which contained the presents for the
Indians, but Brown retook the house and outbuildings with bay-

onets and the siege began: Brown and his King's Rangers in the White House, Creek warriors in outbuildings and behind earthworks they had dug around the perimeter. On the 15th Brown wrote to Cruger at Ninety Six, "your own ideas of my present situation will readily lead you to give such aid as you may judge to be effectual, till which time I shall maintain my post to the last extremity."[3]

Ninety Six was some fifty-two miles due north of Augusta. On September 15 two persons of "credit and veracity" appeared at Ninety Six and told Cruger of Clarke's attack. The following morning Cruger got Brown's letter of the 15th and at 08.00 hours "march'd off a force sufficient . . . to save him." Cruger wrote to Cornwallis an hour later, "I go off this instant and beg your Lordship will pardon this hurried scrawl."[4]

Conditions inside the White House were deplorable. Brown was shot in both thighs but carried on. By the time Cruger reached the scene the besieged were eating raw pumpkins, had been without water for two days, and were reduced to drinking their own cold urine. Cruger's arrival on the morning of September 18, however, dramatically changed the situation. By then Clarke's force had been reduced to about 200, as undisciplined militiamen wandered off in search of plunder and to visit family and friends in the area. Cruger, joined by Brown's King's Rangers and the Indians surged to the attack. After a brief resistance, Clarke and his men abandoned the fight, or as Cruger put it, "went off in the most precipitate manner."[5]

To borrow the title of Steven Rauch's excellent article on Clarke's siege of Augusta, it was indeed "An Ill-Timed and Premature Insurrection." It brought down on the Rebels in Georgia, and especially Wilkes County, the wrath of the British, and we may surmise, as is always the case in such situations, collateral damage, as innocents suffered along with Rebels.

Cruger wrote to Nisbet Balfour, "I am now sending out parties of horse to pick up the traitorous rebels of this neighborhood, who will be roughly handled, some very probably suspended for their good deeds." He was right. Thirteen men were hanged in

Augusta for breaking parole. Others were turned over to the Indians and were either scalped or "thrown into the fires and
roasted to death." Cruger then marched up country in pursuit of
Clarke, and with another purpose in mind. "I meant by this
march also to settle the Ceded Lands business, which I flatter myself will not be very difficult if we drive Clark out of the country,
as all or very near the whole of the inhabitants are with him." That
was on September 23 and about sixty miles north of Augusta. Five
days later he reported that Clarke "had moved on so fast as to get
beyond our reach," apparently headed for refuge in North Carolina. Cruger hoped he could be intercepted, for he had previously written, "If they escape us . . . I am in hopes Ferguson may
cross upon them. I have given him notice."[6]

Clarke and the men still with him had fetched their families
and a refugee column of about 800 people—more than 300 men
and 400 women and children—made their arduous trek into the
mountains and through Cherokee country to refuge among the
Over Mountain people. Cruger, however, wrote that 200 fighting
men "(many with their families) have gone off with Clark." Back
in the Ceded Lands of Wilkes County, those left behind paid the
price for Clarke's "Ill-Timed and Premature Insurrection."
Cruger reported to Cornwallis, "our militia horse have been very
busily employed scouring the country. The rebel courthouse,
forts, and some private houses belonging to the most notorious
villains are burnt, their cattle driven off, and their property in
general paying the price of their treachery." He added that the
militia would "remove and devour what property the absconding
rebels may leave."[7]

By early spring Clarke was east of the mountains again. Readers will recall that in July 1780 Clarke and the Tory Captain James
Dunlop, who was then serving under Major Patrick Ferguson, met
in battle at Cedar Spring, where both were wounded. Eight
months later, March 23, 1781, they faced off at Beattie's Mill in
South Carolina. The promoted Major Dunlop then commanded
the cavalry at Ninety Six. With seventy-six horse and foot, he was
on a foraging expedition when he encountered Elijah Clarke and

about 180 Georgia and South Carolina partisans. Andrew Pickens got the story of what happened from Clarke and reported it to Major General Nathanael Greene. Clarke sent part of his force around Dunlop's to block a retreat, then attacked, wrote Pickens, "with vigour and resolution." Dunlop's cavalry fled, most of "their Horse being chiefly killed in the flight." Dunlop's infantry took shelter in the mill and outbuildings, but Clarke's force poured fire into the buildings. Taking big losses, thirty-four killed, Dunlop surrendered. He was sent with the other forty-two prisoners under guard to Virginia. But in Gilbert Town, North Carolina, Dunlop was murdered by "a set of Men chiefly unknown" who "forced the guard and shot him." Pickens was outraged and offered a reward of $10,000 for the capture of the killers. But the backwoods version of *omerta* settled like a dark haze over the affair, the reward ignored, and nobody was brought to justice.[8]

The next we hear of Clarke, he and his Georgians were with Sumter's band at Fishdam Ford on the night of November 9, 1780, when the Rebel camp was attacked by Major James Wemyss (pronounced weems) (1748–1833), commanding forty dragoons of Tarleton's British Legion and 100 mounted infantry of 63rd Foot. No doubt Clarke greatly enjoyed the British debacle. Caught in the glare of Rebel campfires, the forty dragoons of the British Legion and 100 mounted infantry were repulsed by Rebels firing from the darkness. Two sergeants and twenty rank and file were killed. Wemyss was taken prisoner but later released on parole and exchanged for a Rebel prisoner.[9]

Colonel Clarke and about 100 Georgians were also at the important Battle of Blackstock's on November 20, 1780. There were other senior officers of solid reputations among the Georgians: Colonels John Twiggs and Benjamin Few, and two veterans of King's Mountain, Major James Jackson and Major William Candler.[10]

Cornwallis, determined to deal once and for all with Thomas Sumter, wrote Banastre Tarleton, "we can do no good without you. I trust to your coming immediately unless you see something still more materially pressing." Tarleton came immediately.[11]

At a conference of the senior officers with Sumter, it was decided to take a defensive position on William Blackstock's farm. The farmhouse and outbuildings made of stout logs were on a hill. Behind them a road descended about 200 yards to the Tyger River. In front of them about fifty acres of open land provided clear fields for fire and maneuver. Besides the buildings, there was also a strong fence of small trees. There was plenty of cover for the South Carolina and Georgia riflemen.

Tarleton closed rapidly on Sumter's position with 190 cavalry of the British Legion and 17th Light Dragoons, and 90 infantry of 63rd Foot. He would not have considered it a handicap that he would be going up against Sumter's 1,000 militia. After all, he was a regular and leading regulars. But death rained down on the British ranks as riflemen from South Carolina and Georgia, firing from behind cover, stopped cold the British advance. For the first time in his career, Tarleton had been defeated.[12]

Then he lied about it. He lied in his official report to Cornwallis and he lied in his memoir of the war. He claimed "immediate success," the deaths of three American colonels, and "upwards of one hundred Americans were killed and wounded and fifty were made prisoners." All lies. Tarleton admitted to fifty killed and wounded, but it may have been more.[13]

As always, Clarke did not observe the action from afar but was up front and active. Veterans of the action testified to that in their pension applications. A "British officer cut off the run [rim] of his [Clarke's] hat—and through his epaulette." Leading about thirty men, Clarke was separated from the main body and did not rejoin it until about midnight. Several of his men and Clarke were wounded. Clarke "was shot through the arm but did not break a bone."[14]

From his participation in one of the great partisan victories of the war, a little over three weeks later, December 12, 1780, in a skirmish at Long Cane, Elijah Clarke suffered defeat and a grave wound that kept him out of the Battle of Cowpens, Daniel Morgan's tactical masterpiece of the war in which Banastre Tarleton's bubble was burst for good. A small group of Georgians, commanded by Major James Jackson, fought at the battle under Andrew Pickens.

Aside from Indian fighting on the frontier, Elijah Clarke's last hurrah in the war was at the second siege of Augusta, May 23 to June 5, 1780. Once again the foe was the hated Colonel Thomas "Burntfoot" Brown, his King's Carolina Rangers, and his Indian allies. Clarke began the siege, but it was soon taken over by others. The total Rebel force numbered some 1,500 regulars and militia: about 468 Continentals of Lieutenant Colonel Henry "Light Horse Harry" Lee's Legion; about 550 South Carolina militia commanded by Brigadier General Andrew Pickens; and about 500 of Clarke's Georgia militia. Even though the number of men he brought to the fight was on a par with the other leaders, in this action Clarke played second fiddle to Pickens and Lee. Pickens was the senior militia officer present. Lee as a Continental officer took precedence over both Clarke and Pickens, but he and Pickens worked well together and made the big decisions. After "a judicious and gallant defense," Brown surrendered, but only he, Lee, and Pickens signed the articles of surrender. Indeed, the mutual loathing between Brown and Clarke was so strong that the historian of the second siege reasonably commented that Brown might not have signed had Clarke's name—or E, which he had become capable of printing—appeared on the document.[15]

Light Horse Harry Lee, Virginia gentry, always conscious of his standing far above those whom John Adams referred to as the "common Herd of Mankind," loathed Clarke's militia. They "[exc]eed Goths & Vandals in their schemes of plunder murder & iniqu[ity]," he wrote to Greene, and urged his general "to govern this state, till civil government can be introduced." Greene had begun an effort to bring order to the Georgia Back Country before Lee made his plea, writing to Elijah Clarke on May 29 of the need to establish a permanent force, similar to a Continental regiment, to serve at least twelve months, and whose troops would receive the same "pay and Clothing" as Continental soldiers. Clarke, Greene continued, would have the authority to appoint officers and command the regiment until a governor was functioning and should make his "pleasure" known. He also stressed that an "arrangement of the Georgia Militia is absolutely necessary for the protection of the good people in that State." Pay "attention to that business," Greene added. If Clarke replied, it has not been found, and I think it safe to presume that he took no action on the matter.[16]

It was a losing battle. Lee was biased but he was right. As Dr. Thomas Taylor, a Tory surgeon, wrote, "Putting a man to Death in cold blood is very prettily nicknamed giving a Georgia parole."[17]

The Revolutionary War ended with the signing of the Peace of Paris in 1783. Now the time had come for men who had been fighting for eight years to set aside their arms and turn to plow and pen. Peacetime, however, was largely downhill for Elijah Clarke, and at the end disastrous. At first he prospered both financially and politically. As a reward for his Revolutionary services, Georgia gave him the confiscated estate of his Tory neighbor, Colonel Thomas Waters. The state had given land grants to veterans, and Clarke bought so many of the bounty certificates that he acquired thousands of acres. But the war services of veterans had to be certified before the certificates were issued, only Clarke had certified many men's services, and "Some of the men he vouched for as Patriots even appear to have been members of [Burntfoot] Brown's King's Rangers!" But criticism of his actions did not prevent him from playing important roles in the early aftermath of the war.[18]

Clarke was a member of the Georgia legislature representing Wilkes County from 1781 to 1790, served on committees as well as the commission for confiscated Tory estates, and was also a commissioner at almost all of Georgia's Indian treaties. In 1781 he was elected by the legislature as colonel of the Wilkes County militia, five years later brigadier general, and in 1792 major general.

In 1787, learning of two Indian attacks, Clarke set out on what he was best at. He "collected 160 men, chiefly volunteers," and set out on the trail of an Indian band that had killed three men and "found the bodies . . . mangled in a shocking manner, and after I had buried them, proceeded on the trail of the murderers." Unable to catch up with that band, Clarke happened on a "fresh trail of Indians coming towards our frontier settlements," and followed their trail until he "came up with them" on the morning of September 21 "between eleven and twelve o'clock" at a branch of the Ocmulgee River called Jack's Creek that the Indians had just crossed. After passing through a thick canebrake, the Indians had camped on a hill, started a fire, and were cooking food. By then Clarke's force had dwindled to 130, as the horses of some had given out. Clarke deployed, attacked, drove the Indians into the canebrake, and firing was exchanged until 4:30 p.m. During that time Indians escaped by small groups. At sunset Clarke withdrew to care for his eleven wounded. Six of his men were killed, but he was certain of "not less than twenty-five Indians killed" and their provisions and belongings, including "thirty-two brass kettles, thirty-seven large packs, containing blankets," captured.[19]

Seven years later there appeared on Clarke's horizon a Frenchman who was young, brash, and ignorant of the United States and its government. Unfortunately, Edmund Charles Genet (1763–1834) was also the French minister to the young Republic. France was then at war with Britain and European powers, including Spain. Appointed by the Girondins, then in control of the French revolutionary government, he believed as they did in universal revolution, what they called the "empire of liberty." In their naiveté, the Girondins thought that since France was now a republic, and the United States a republic, the two republics would naturally join hands to fight Britain and Spain and spread republicanism. In their ignorance, Girondins also thought that foreign policy lay within Congress' domain, and Genet's letter of accreditation was to Congress, not the President. When Genet realized that he had to deal with President Washington and met him, he developed an instant dislike for the great man and thought him "a pompous old fool."[20]

Citizen Genet, as he called himself, was instructed by his government to demand of the American government that under the treaties signed by the two countries in 1778, when they became allies against Great Britain during the Revolutionary War, France could base privateers in American ports to attack British ships and bring their prizes into those ports; recruit an American army to invade East Florida, once more held by Spain; and recruit another force of Americans to invade Spanish-held Louisiana. Such actions, of course, would be a violation of President Washington's wise policy of strict neutrality in the European wars. The brash young man's instructions also included a demand that the United States quickly pay back the loans France had made to America during the Revolutionary War. Compounding these demands, Genet's behavior was outrageous. He went over the heads of President Washington, Secretary of State Jefferson, indeed, the entire American government, and assured his superiors in Paris that he had the support of the American people "in spite of their stupid government." Thomas Jefferson, pro-French to his core, tried to counsel young Genet, to no avail. He vented his anger toward Genet in a letter to James Madison: "Never in my opinion was so calamitous an appointment made, as that of the present minister of F. here."[21]

This was the man who put Elijah Clarke on the French payroll at a salary of $10,000 and a major general's commission to raise a force of Georgians and invade Spanish East Florida. Clarke and his fellow frontiersmen were willing and eager.[22]

Clarke resigned his Georgia militia Major General's commission on February 18, 1794. Three days later he wrote to a French agent in Charleston that it was "the prettiest time imaginable to lead men to great achievements. . . . My hopes are buoyed up to a higher pitch than ever they were in my life." But all of their hopes and ambitions fizzled when President Washington called for Genet's recall and the new French government, now under the Jacobins, complied. (We are not, however, done with Edmund Charles Genet and will meet him later when another of our Colonels becomes involved in French machinations.) Elijah

Clarke, no longer a major general in the French service, turned his sole attention to another matter that had been festering in his mind since 1790, as it had in the minds of all frontiersmen.[23]

In that year a large delegation of Creek leaders traveled one thousand miles to New York City, then the nation's capital, and there on August 7, 1790, Secretary of War Henry Knox, the famous Creek mixed blood leader Alexander McGillivary, and twenty-three Creek chiefs signed the Treaty of New York. The Creeks gave up three million acres in Georgia between the Ogeechee and Oconee Rivers. But all of the country west and south of the Oconee were guaranteed by the federal government to be Creek lands. In other words, most of modern-day Georgia was Indian country, and any non-Indian who "shall attempt to settle on any of the Creek lands . . . shall forfeit the protection of the United States, and the Creeks may punish him or not, as they please."[24]

Elijah Clarke was furious, his fellow frontiersmen were furious, and neither Clarke nor they had any intention of obeying a document hatched back east. Major Robert Flournoy, a man of some substance who lived west of the Oconee, wrote in October 1793 to James Seagrove, Superintendent of Indian Affairs for the South, "you strongly adhere to that destructive principle of our Northeastwardly politicians. Make peace on any terms say they; it is that disposition in our Northern brethren, which was so plainly delivered to the Indians . . . at New York, that has brought all the evils on this country that we have since experienced." Three months later the *Augusta Chronicle* spelled out in plain English what the frontiersmen wanted and how to do it. "Nothing short of the extirpation of the Creek and Cherokee nations will ensure peace to the frontiers, and it here appears much easier to do it than to obtain an order from the government to have it done."[25]

The hunger of frontiersmen for land and their unrestrained methods of taking it were of long standing. James Wright, the last British royal governor of Georgia, found it "not to be in my power to restrain men at so great a distance from me, from committing some outrages, or from taking satisfaction themselves. . . . You know perfectly well what sort of people live in these parts of the country." It would be no different under American governors. Seagrove reported to the governor of Georgia that on September 15, 1793, a band of frontiersmen crossed the Oconee, penetrated over 100 miles to a small Creek town on the Chatahoochee River, killed and scalped six Creek men, brought back eight women as prisoners, and "plundered and burnt the town."[26]

After the East Florida invasion was cancelled, in the spring and summer of 1794 Elijah Clarke led his followers across the Oconee and organized "A Separate and Independent Government," what historians would call the Trans-Oconee Republic. They wrote a constitution, formed a committee of safety, elected officers, and for seventy miles along the western bank of the Oconee River established several settlements and built six forts. Directly across the river from the federal Fort Fidius was the new government's Fort Advance. In May 1794, James Seagrove wrote to Governor Matthews (1739–1812) that he was devastated "to see the fruit of my labors destroyed in a moment, by the rash and lawless conduct of individuals."[27]

Governor Matthews investigated, warned, waffled, finally issued a proclamation against Clarke's actions, and hoped the courts could handle the matter. Clarke returned to the eastern side of the Oconee and went before a superior court judge who also waffled. He sent Clarke to a panel of judges who proceeded to publicly declare their sympathies, writing that "after a most mature consideration . . . and examination of the laws . . . we give it as our decided and unanimous opinion, that said Elijah Clarke be and is hereby discharged," whereupon Clarke returned to his new home on the west bank of the Oconee. Constant Freeman, an agent for the federal Department of War in Georgia, reported that "This decision greatly encouraged his party, and the settlements were pushed with vigor."[28]

The Revolution had ended a little over a decade before. A constitution had been written and ratified by the states. A national government, not without trial and error and pain, was asserting itself. Yet Elijah Clarke refused to recognize either state or federal authority and forged ahead, asserting the beliefs and desires of himself and his fellow frontiersmen. But when President Washington heard by July 1794 of the settlements west of the Oconee, he ordered them removed.

Governor Matthews then ordered the militia to remove the settlers from Creek lands. On September 29 Constant Freeman reported to Secretary of War Henry Knox: "I have the pleasure to inform you, that the post [Fort Advance] opposite us [Fort Fidius], on the south side of the Oconee, has been taken and destroyed by the militia, and that General Clarke and his adherents have been removed." By October 1 the settlements were also destroyed. Elijah Clarke's Trans-Oconee Republic was no more.[29]

Clarke was in such a funk that some two months later he wrote to an acquaintance in Kentucky about land there, stating that many of his followers "would rather live a hunter's life in the bleak mountains than continue on where they are," and added, "I am disgusted with this State." His mood, however, did not stop him in 1795 from again organizing another plot to attack Spanish East Florida, but United States and Spanish forces put a stop to that. Another failed endeavor.[30]

Elijah Clarke was a warrior. He was not meant for peacetime life. "A few years before his death, Clarke wrote to a friend about how much he longed to return to the uninhibited frontier life he had known as a young man."[31]

Colonel Elijah Clarke, hero of the Revolution, died in Augusta on December 5, 1799, age 57, disillusioned, reputation diminished, pursued by creditors, unknown today.

## COLONEL ISAAC SHELBY

We have seen Colonel Shelby's prominent role in the King's Mountain Campaign. Some writers credit him with planning, in concert with Nathanael Greene and Daniel Morgan, the campaign that led to the subsequent game-changing Battle of Cowpens, and that he was at the battle. I have found no evidence for the former, and he certainly was not at Cowpens.[32]

His next venture east of the mountains came late in the war at the behest of Major General Nathanael Greene. In June 1781

Greene urged Shelby and the other prominent Over Mountain leader, Colonel John Sevier (1745–1815), to join him in South Carolina. Both men, however, had other pressing responsibilities. Shelby wrote that taking fighting men eastward would leave the frontier "greatly exposed" until a treaty could be made with the Cherokee. The harvest was also at hand. By August it seemed that Shelby was ready to march with 700 "good rifle men well mounted." But both the length of their absence and the danger of disease during the "Sickly Season" led to the refusal of Shelby's militia to march. They would not join their Rebel comrades in South Carolina "untill the fall season." Shelby joined Francis Marion by November 2.[33]

Shelby and his men did not stay long. They participated in at least one operation under the command of one of Marion's subordinates, Colonel Hezekiah Maham. Marion wrote to Greene that "Col Maham gives Col Shelby the greatest Applause for his readyness and the good order he kept his men." The swampy Low Country, however, was not to the liking of the Over Mountain Men. It is reasonable to speculate that they were unhappy, wanted to go home, and pressed Shelby on the matter. In the same letter in which Marion passed on Colonel Maham's praise of Shelby, he also wrote, "Col Shelby has my permission to retire to N Carolina." By November 27 he reported that the "mountaineers" had gone home.[34]

Unlike Elijah Clarke, following the war Isaac Shelby went on to an esteemed national reputation, high political office, and more military glory. Following his brief service in General Greene's army in South Carolina's Low Country, he returned to the lands beyond the mountains and set out for the country he had long considered home—Kentucky—and there began to build a house on the land he had previously claimed. Shelby eventually owned 6,000 acres, which he worked with servants and slaves. Shelby's lifelong interest in the land led to his helping to organize and become the first president of the Kentucky Society for Promoting Useful Arts, which was established to promote agricultural education and information about farming and animal husbandry. On April 19, 1783, age thirty-two, he married nine-teen-year-old Susannah Hart, of a well-to-do North Carolina family. Isaac and Susannah had eleven children.[35]

Politics would claim much of his time and service. Kentucky was then part of Virginia. The populace ranged from squatter to planter. Most of the population was from Appalachia, but a strong element came from the coastal and piedmont areas of Virginia. Among the latter were movers and shakers who favored Kentucky remaining part of Virginia. Isaac Shelby "supported their position." He would also oppose the new federal Constitution, believing with others that it gave too much power to the federal government—a theme continuing into our times.[36]

Although to what degree is uncertain, Shelby was apparently involved in a scheme that led some to urge that Kentucky leave the Union and ally itself with Spain, perhaps even becoming a Spanish colony. It is a tangled tale whose intricacies need not detain us except to present an outline and Shelby's role in what is known to history as the Spanish Conspiracy, although the historian A. P. Whitaker suggested that it be called the Frontier Conspiracy, since it originated not with Spaniards but American frontiersmen. Under the terms of the Peace of Paris of 1783, ending the Revolutionary War, Britain gave the United States most of the lands west of the Appalachians. Spain, however, held Florida and Louisiana, had posts on the Mississippi from Natchez to St. Louis, and claimed most of the territory Britain had handed over to its former colonies, even the southwestern corner of Kentucky. At the heart of the matter were navigation rights on the Mississippi River. The treaty gave Americans the right to navigate the entire length of the great river. But Spain refused to recognize Article 8 of the treaty and closed the Mississippi to Americans, denying Kentuckians entrée to New Orleans and a marketplace to the world. Of course, at this early date there was little commerce west of Appalachia, but Kentuckians were looking to the future. Westerners were in an uproar.[37]

The great scoundrel of the early Republic, James Wilkinson, Agent No. 13 of the Spanish crown, convinced some Kentuckians that their future lay with Spain. In a petition to Spanish authorities written in New Orleans, Wilkinson asked for pensions for several people, including $800 for Isaac Shelby and another "man of influence," who along with others, wrote Wilkinson, "favor separation from the United States and a friendly connection with Spain." Can we believe Wilkinson? He was a serial liar and a traitor, but . . . In the end, Wilkinson's treasonous activities came to nothing, the "conspiracy" had no marked effect on the development of the western lands, and Isaac Shelby, known in Kentucky as "Old King's Mountain," retained the reputation he had built during the Revolution and went on to more military glory.[38]

Meanwhile, opposition to governance by Virginia did not go away. Because of Virginia's policy prohibiting offensive operations against the Indians, Isaac Shelby changed his mind, supported "separation from Virginia," became a major player, and was elected to the Kentucky Constitutional Convention. On June 1, 1792, Kentucky became the fifteenth State of the Union, and on June 4 Isaac Shelby, age forty-one, became the first governor of Kentucky.[39]

What we might call the French Conspiracy on the Mississippi took place during Isaac Shelby's first governorship. At the center of a plot to recruit Kentuckians to seize Spanish posts of the Mississippi and take New Orleans was none other than Elijah Clarke's French connection, Citizen Genet. But Spain got wind of the plot, complained to President George Washington, and on August 29, 1793, Secretary of State Thomas Jefferson wrote Governor Shelby that he was charged by the "President" with regard to the plotters "that . . . you take those legal measures which shall be necessary to prevent any such enterprise."[40]

Shelby replied on October 5 that he was "persuaded, at present, none such is in contemplation in this place." Jefferson, however, wrote again on November 9 naming four French agents planning such an enterprise and asking Shelby if necessary to use the militia to stop any such expedition. Shelby claimed that he did not receive Jefferson's letters until late December. Yet he surely knew what was going on. Arthur St. Clair (pronounced Sinclair), governor of the Northwest Territory, wrote Shelby on November

7, 1793, that "I have received pretty direct information . . . that General [George Rogers] Clark has received a commission from the government of France, and is about to raise a body of men in Kentucky to attack the Spanish settlements on the Mississippi." Then, in late November, Shelby heard directly from two of the French agents named by Jefferson, writing not from long distance but Knob Lick, Kentucky, only some 100 miles from the state capital of Frankfort. They both addressed Shelby as "Citizen Governor" and one admitted that he had come to join the expedition on the Mississippi. A historian of the affair believed that Shelby preferred "watchful waiting rather than to employ an aggressive policy of military suppression." But another historian, in a fine study of the crises of the 1790s, wrote that Shelby's "message was clear—and disturbing: as governor, he could ignore the federal government's diplomatic alliances if and when he chose to do so." A little over three months after his letter of October 5 of the previous year in which he had stated that he would "prevent any such attempts of that nature," on January 13, 1794, Shelby wrote to Jefferson contradicting that letter.[41]

"I have great doubts even if they do attempt to carry their plan into execution (provided they manage their business with prudence) whether there is any legal authority to restrain or punish them, at least before they have actually accomplished it." Thus he revealed his true colors. Isaac Shelby sympathized with the plotters. He was a westerner, and with his fellow westerners distrusted authorities in the east to uphold the interests of the west, at that time principally navigation rights on the Mississippi.[42]

Shelby's defiance led to a March 10, 1794, cabinet meeting called by President George Washington for an "Opinion on Expeditions Being Planned In Kentucky for the Invasion of the Spanish Dominions." On March 24 Washington issued a strong "Proclamation on Expeditions" that ended Citizen Genet's pipe dreams. Governor Isaac Shelby was later attacked by his political enemies for his refusal to arrest the plotters.[43]

As for Citizen Genet, American diplomatic efforts led to his recall by the French government, where power had shifted from the Girondin party to the Jacobin party. Genet would have been guillotined by the radical Jacobins now ruling France, so the Washington administration allowed him to stay. He did well for himself, becoming a U.S. citizen and marrying Cornelia Clinton, the wealthy daughter of George Clinton, governor of New York and vice president of the United States. Cornelia died in 1810, and four years later he married Martha Brandon Osgood, another member of the American establishment, daughter of the Postmaster General, Samuel Osgood. With his two wives, Citizen Genet had ten children and lived out his life as a country gentleman on his farm overlooking the Hudson River.

Shelby retired after his first term and returned to the home he called Traveler's Rest and peaceful pursuits. With the outbreak of the War of 1812, however, he was prevailed on to run for another term as governor. He won handily, and at the age of sixty-two Isaac Shelby went to war for the third time in his life.

For the most part, the dramatic actions of the western theater of the War of 1812 took place in northwestern Ohio, the adjacent southeastern corner of Michigan, and adjoining Canada. (Michigan was not then a state but part of the Indiana Territory.) Under the terms of the Peace of Paris of 1783 that ended the Revolutionary War, the British had ceded to the United States the area that would become the states of Ohio, Indiana, Illinois, Michigan, Wisconsin, and the eastern part of Minnesota. On July 13, 1787, Congress passed the Northwest Ordinance that established the Northwest Territory. (When Ohio became a state in 1803, the rest of the area became the Indiana Territory.) But this huge area was also the home of powerful Indian nations, and the British fudged on the cession, supported their Indian allies, and aimed at holding on to Detroit and preventing the Americans from establishing themselves throughout the Old Northwest. Among the American goals in the War of 1812 were to expel the British from land that they believed rightfully theirs, subdue the Indians, and the same as in the east, take Canada—the latter goal tilting at windmills wherever it occurred.

On January 22, 1813, an army of some 1,000 men, mostly Kentuckians, at Frenchtown (modern Monroe) on the river Raisin just south of Detroit, was surprised and overrun by a British and Indian army. An astute historian of the War of 1812 rightly accused the American commander of "nearly criminal neglect." Several prisoners were killed by Indians. British officers watching the killings did not intervene. Some eighty wounded prisoners were left behind without an armed guard after the British marched off. About thirty Kentuckians were killed, either by burning to death in houses the Indians set afire or killed while trying to escape the flames. The cry of "Remember the River Raisin" echoed throughout Kentucky.[44]

The commanding general of American forces in the west, William Henry Harrison (1773–1841), one of the few competent American generals of the war, called upon Governor Shelby for reinforcements, as his regiments were well below authorized strength. Harrison's appointment to command had largely been the result of pressure brought to bear on Washington by Isaac Shelby and other prominent Kentuckians. Harrison and Shelby would work together seamlessly. Harrison asked Shelby to come in person, and added, "I have such confidence in your wisdom that you in fact should 'be the guiding Head and I the hand.'" Shelby replied, "had I more age & much greater experience I would not hesitate to fight under your banner for the honour and interest of my beloved country."[45]

"Old King's Mountain" immediately issued a statewide call "for a general rendezvous of KENTUCKY VOLUNTEERS" on August 31, 1813, at Newport, Kentucky, across the Ohio River from Cincinnati, and wrote, "I will meet you there in person. I will lead you to the field of battle, and share with you the dangers and honors of the campaign." When Shelby reviewed his militia force at Newport, from his hip was suspended the sword awarded to him by the North Carolina legislature for the great Revolutionary War victory at King's Mountain. Without wasting time, Shelby led his men across the Ohio on the day they mustered and set out for a rendezvous with Harrison. On September 14, at the head of about 3,000 Kentucky militia, Shelby joined Harrison on the Portage River in northern Ohio, east of present-day Sandusky.[46]

Two days earlier General Harrison had received the famous message from Commodore Oliver Hazard Perry, announcing his key naval victory on Lake Erie: "We have met the enemy, and they are ours: two ships, two brigs, one schooner, and one sloop." Dominance of Lake Erie meant the way was clear for Harrison to invade Canada and seek battle with General Henry Proctor's British army and his Indian allies led by the great Tecumseh. On September 27, in nine vessels and about eighty boats, the army proceeded across Lake Erie to land in Canada at the mouth of the Detroit River. Isaac Shelby commanded the right wing of Harrison's army. After landing, Harrison considered moving the army forward on Lake Erie to get behind Proctor and consulted Shelby and Perry. Both were opposed. Perry told Harrison that in October the waters and high winds made navigation dangerous, and Shelby and his men, landlubbers all, had more than enough of sailing and rowing. Harrison accepted their objections and the pursuit of Proctor's army proceeded by land.[47]

On October 5, 1813, the Battle of the Thames took place at Moraviantown, Canada, on the Thames River some eighty miles northeast of Detroit. On the morning of the 5th, Harrison was with the advance of mounted Kentuckians commanded by Colonel Richard Johnson. Isaac Shelby commanded the infantry and was ordered to bring them on as quickly as possible. The seasoned campaigner did better. He drove the infantry hard and kept up with Johnson's horsemen. Thereafter, he was in the thick of it. As the battle raged and the outcome hung in the balance, Shelby ordered the reserves forward, sent a regiment to support Colonel Johnson's horsemen, and directed a brigade to close up the front.[48]

The Battle of the Thames was hardly a storied battle. It lasted perhaps three quarters of an hour and ended with a British defeat. Its most celebrated event was the death in battle of the great Tecumseh. But its consequences for the United States and the Indians of the Northwest were beyond significant. Detroit had been retaken and would remain American, and Michigan was safe. Even more important, in the absence of British support no longer would the Indians of the region prevent American possession of the Old Northwest. Not long after the war, hordes of settlers would see to that.[49]

In 1780 Isaac Shelby had played key roles in the Battle of Musgrove's Mill and in the subsequent campaign that led to the pivotal battle of King's Mountain. In 1813 the campaign and battle that sealed American hegemony in the Old Northwest would not have been possible without his support and participation. For his role in the Battle of the Thames, Congress passed a resolution awarding Shelby a Congressional Medal.

Isaac Shelby finished his term as governor in 1816 and retired to Traveler's Rest. The following year President James Monroe asked Shelby to become Secretary of War. He declined because of his advanced age. Isaac Shelby died on July 18, 1826, fourteen days after the July 4 deaths of Thomas Jefferson and John Adams. On August 15 of that year, a fellow Kentuckian, William T. Barry, who would become Postmaster General in President Andrew Jackson's cabinet, at a time when that was a powerful political position, gave a speech in Lexington. It was entitled *Speech of William T. Barry, Esq. on the Deaths of Adams, Jefferson, and Shelby*. Thus was "Old King's Mountain" joined with two Founders and recognized for the high esteem in which he was held throughout the nation.

## COLONEL JAMES WILLIAMS

James Williams was mortally wounded on October 7, 1780, leading his troops as they gained the crest at King's Mountain and died the following the day. Thomas Young, a veteran militia fighter at age sixteen, was there and in his memoir probably gave the most accurate description of Williams' death in battle.

> On the top of the mountain, in the thickest of the fight, I saw Colonel Williams fall, and a braver man never died upon the field of battle. I had seen him but once before on that day: it was in the beginning of the action as he charged by me at full speed around the mountain. Toward the summit, a ball struck his horse's under jaw. Colonel Williams threw the reins over the animal's neck, sprang to the ground and dashed on-

ward. The moment I heard the cry that Colonel Williams was shot, I ran to his assistance—for I loved him as a brother—he had been ever so kind to me, almost always carrying a cake in his pocket for me and his little son, Joseph. They carried him into a tent and sprinkled some water in his face. As he revived his first words were: "For God's sake, boys, don't give up the hill!" I remember it as if it had occurred yesterday. I left him in the arms of his son, Daniel, and returned to the field to avenge his fall.[50]

But Colonel Williams' tale was not over. In 1814, Colonel William Hill, a devoted follower of Thomas Sumter, wrote his memoirs and in it blackened Colonel Williams' name for two centuries. Historians and writers since accepted Hill as gospel in their assessments of Williams, and I must admit that I am one of them. Mea culpa! One hundred and ninety-eight years later a historian, William T. Graves, in a book graced by excellent research, rescued Williams from undeserved anonymity and, most importantly, recovered his reputation.[51]

We noted in the section on James Williams' background in Chapter 2 that a split occurred between Williams and Sumter and that both Lord Cornwallis and Governor Rutledge were aware of it. Cornwallis described it as a "quarrel . . . over command," and Rutledge wrote that the two men "will never agree." Will Graves has pointed out that the Rebels in Sumter's camp came from different areas of the South Carolina Back Country, and their primary interest was to protect their home areas from the British and the Tory militia. Sumter and his followers, including William Hill, were from the central and upper part of the South Carolina Back Country. Williams and the men who followed him were from the western area around the British post of Ninety Six, where enemy patrols were active.[52]

Whatever the specific reason(s) for their split, Colonel Williams and his followers left Sumter's camp sometime in late July–early August and made their way to Colonel Charles McDowell's bivouac at Smith's Ford on the Broad River where Williams would team with Colonels Elijah Clarke and Isaac Shelby. Will

Graves quotes Sumter's major—and not uncritical—biographer, Anne King Gregorie.

> On the march to the Waxhaws, Sumter was joined by his Commissary, Colonel James Williams. While encamped at Cane Creek, it was agreed that Williams should take such of the troops as would accompany him and march through the region now comprised in the counties of York, Spartanburg, and Laurens. At the same time Sumter should descend the Wateree and co-operate with Gates, who was advancing through the pine barrens toward Camden.[53]

Major Joseph McJunkin recalled the separation in the same light as Will Graves. "About this time, Col James Williams joined Sumter—the latter having a disposition to go Southward, & the former towards the West. Disagreeing in their notions, the troops joined with Sumter or Williams just as their own inclinations led them."[54]

Gregorie added that Williams "made off" with some horses and other supplies and that this led to the dispute between Williams and Sumter. "Made off"? As Will Graves asked, how does one campaign without horses, ammunition, and supplies? Plus, Williams' followers were men of honor and standing in their communities and had their own followers who went with them: Thomas Brandon, Joseph Hayes, James Steen, Joseph McJunkin, and Samuel Hammond. Brandon, McJunkin, and Hammond would serve under Williams at Musgrove's Mill.[55]

In his memoir, William Hill listed six baseless accusations against Colonel James Williams: He deserted Sumter and embezzled supplies; confronted, he promised to return the supplies but reneged; he took undeserved credit for the victory at Musgrove's Mill; he attempted to divert to his home district Patriot forces gathering to fight Major Patrick Ferguson; he played an unwelcome and minor role in the Battle of King's Mountain; he was killed shortly after the battle by one of his own men.[56]

Each charge was a lie, and Will Graves proves it in *Backcountry Revolutionary: James Williams (1740–1780) with Source Documents*. I highly recommend it.

James Williams was partially rescued from oblivion in the early twentieth and early twenty-first centuries. In 1917, what were believed to be his remains were disinterred, placed in an iron chest, and reburied in front of the Cherokee County Administration Building in Gaffney, South Carolina. The site is marked by a memorial erected by the Daughters of the American Revolution.[57]

In 2005, the South Carolina legislature confirmed James Williams as a brigadier general, a rank he may have received 225 years before, although no evidence of a contemporary promotion has been found. In the same act, on the northeastern corner of what had been Williams' plantation, the legislature renamed the Little River Bridge the "James Williams Memorial Bridge."

# Appendix A

## American Order of Battle (200)
### Musgrove's Mill, August 19, 1780

NORTH CAROLINA MILITIA—Colonel Isaac Shelby
    Sullivan County Militia (Over Mountain Men)
        Lieutenant Colonel Charles Robertson (6 companies)
        Captain Joseph Culbertson
        Captain Valentine Sevier, Jr.
        Captain Major Parson (from South Carolina)
        Captain Joseph Roddy
        Captain George Taylor
        Captain Thomas Wallace
    Mounted Militia
        Captain Josiah Culbertson
    Washington County Militia (Over Mountain Men)
        Major Jonathan Tipton (7 companies)
        Captain William Bean
        Captain Godfrey Isbell
        Captain John McNabb
        Captain John Stinson

Appendices A and B are the work of Ed Forte with input from John Allison, Charles Baxley, Bruce Bennett, C. Leon Harris, Jeff Kline, and David Reuwer. I made a few changes, especially with regard to numbers engaged. Otherwise, I accept their findings and am indebted to Ed and his colleagues. Todd Braisted helped with some individuals on the Loyalist side, and especially with provincial units. In Appendix B, I did not include the Ninety Six District Brigade of Tory militia in the Order of Battle because it was not at Musgrove's Mill when the battle took place.

    Captain John McCampbell
    Captain William Trimble
    Captain Thomas Price
  Burke County Militia
    Major Joseph McDowell (1 company)
    Captain David Vance

GEORGIA MILITIA—Colonel Elijah Clarke
  Wilkes County Militia (Detachment)
    Captain Shadrach Inman

SOUTH CAROLINA MILITIA—Colonel James Williams
    Major Samuel Hammond
  Little River District Militia
    Lieutenant Colonel Joseph Hayes (4 companies)
    Captain Samuel Farrow
    Captain Robert Gillam, Jr.
    Captain Josiah Greer
    Captain John Ridgeway, Sr.
  1st Spartan Regiment of Militia (Detachment)
    Major Josiah Culbertson/Major William Smith
    (2 companies)
    Captain John Collins
    Captain William Smith
  Lower (Dutch Fork) District Company of Militia
    Captain Jacob Former
  2nd Spartan Regiment (also known as Fair Forest Regiment)
    Colonel Thomas Brandon/
    Lieutenant Colonel James Steen (7 companies)
    Captain Andrew Barry
    Captain Benjamin Jolly
    Captain John Lindsay
    Captain Joseph McJunkin
    Captain Hugh Means
    Captain Moses White
    Captain William White

Roebuck's 2nd Battalion, 1st Spartan Regiment
    Colonel Benjamin Roebuck (4 companies)
    Captain Samuel Peden
    Captain George Roebuck
    Captain Dennis Tramell
    Captain Moses Wood

# Appendix B

Provincial/Tory Order of Battle (264)
Musgrove's Mill, August 19, 1780

Colonel Alexander Innes

PROVINCIAL UNITS

South Carolina Royalists (Detachment) (50)
Major Thomas Fraser
3rd Battalion, Light Company, New Jersey Volunteers (50)
Captain Peter Campbell
Lieutenant William Chew
Lieutenant John Camp
1st Battalion, DeLancey's Brigade (Detachment) (50)
Captain George Kerr

TORY MILITIA—Colonel Daniel Clary
Dutch Fork Regiment (Detachment) (100)
Captain William Hawsey
Captain Vachel Clary
Captain William Ballentine
Captain Humphrey Williamson
Captain George Stroup
Captain James Wright
Captain William Thompson
Fanning's Loyalist Militia (14)
Captain David Fanning

# Notes

Abbreviations used in the notes

| | |
|---|---|
| Allaire | *Diary of Lieut Anthony Allaire, of Ferguson's Corps,* in Draper, below |
| *ASP, IA* | *American State Papers, Indian Affairs,* Class II, 2 vols. (Washington, DC: Gales and Seaton, 1832–1861) |
| Berkin | Carol Berkin, *A Sovereign People: The Crises of the 1790s and the Birth of American Nationalism* (New York: Basic Books, 2017) |
| Bridges | Ed Bridges, "To Establish a Separate and Independent Government," *Furman Review* (Spring Term, 1974) |
| Cashin | Edward J. Cashin, *The King's Ranger: Thomas Brown and the American Revolution on the Southern Frontier* (Athens: University of Georgia Press, 1989) |
| Collins | James Potter Collins, *Autobiography of a Revolutionary Soldier* (1859), in *Sixty Years in the Nueces Valley, 1870–1930* (San Antonio: Naylor Printing Co., 1930) |
| *CP* | *The Cornwallis Papers: The Campaign of 1780 and 1781 in the Southern Theater of the American Revolutionary War,* 6 vols., ed. Ian Saberton (Uckfield: Naval and Military Press, 2010) |
| *DAR* | *Documents of the American Revolution, 1770–1783* (Colonial Office Series), 21 vols., ed. K. G. Davies (Shannon: Irish University Press, 1972–1981) |
| Davis | Robert Scott Davis, "Elijah Clarke: Georgia's Partisan Titan," *SCAR*, 4, nos. 1–3 (January–March 2007), 38–40 |

| | |
|---|---|
| Draper | Lyman C. Draper, *King's Mountain and Its Heroes: The Battle of King's Mountain, October 7, 1780, and the Events Which Led to It* (Scholar's Choice, n.p., n.d.) |
| *GCH* | John Buchanan, *The Road to Guilford Courthouse: The American Revolution in the Carolinas* (New York: John Wiley & Sons, 1997) |
| Graves | William T. Graves, *Backcountry Revolutionary: James Williams (1740–1780) with Source Documents* (Lugoff, SC: Southern Campaigns of the Southern Campaigns Press, 2012) |
| Hammond | Hammond's Account, in Graves (see above) |
| Henderson | Archibald Henderson, "Isaac Shelby and the Genet Mission," *Mississippi Historical Review* 6, no. 4 (March 1920) |
| Hiatt | John Hiatt, *Musgrove Mill State Historic Site: Historic Resource Study* (Columbia: South Carolina State Park Service, May 2000) |
| Johnson | *Captured at Kings Mountain: The Journal of Uzal Johnson*, ed. Wade S. Kolb III and Robert M. Weir (Columbia: University of South Carolina Press, 2011) |
| Johnston | Joseph Johnston, *Traditions and Reminiscences Chiefly of the American Revolution in the South: Including Biographical Sketches, Incidents and Anecdotes* (Charleston: Walker & James, 1851) |
| *JSH* | *Journal of Southern History* |
| Lambert | Robert Stansbury Lambert, *South Carolina Loyalists in the American Revolution* (Columbia: University of South Carolina Press, 1987) |
| Lessons | Robert Scott Davis, "Lessons from Kettle Creek: Patriotism and Loyalism at Askance on the Southern Frontier," *Journal of Backcountry Studies* (online), I: 1 (May 2006) |
| Logan | John H. Logan, *A History of the Upper Country of South Carolina, From the Earliest Periods to the Close of the War of Independence*, vols. I & II (Spartanburg, SC: Reprint Company, 2009) |

| | |
|---|---|
| *Loyalist Corps* | Thomas B. Allen and Todd W. Braisted, *The Loyalist Corps: Americans in the Service of the King* (Takoma Park, MD: Fox Acre Press, 2011) |
| "Notes" | Todd Braisted, "Notes for Jack Buchanan" |
| *PNG* | *The Papers of General Nathanael Greene,* ed. Dennis M. Conrad et al.,13 vols. (Chapel Hill: University of North Carolina Press, 1976–2005) |
| Quimby | Robert S. Quimby, *The U.S. Army in the War of 1812: An Operational and Command Study,* 2 vols. (East Lansing: Michigan State University Press, 1997) |
| *RTC* | John Buchanan, *The Road to Charleston: Nathanael Greene and the American Revolution* (Charlottesville: University Press of Virginia, 2019) |
| *SCAR* | *Journal of the Southern Campaigns of the American Revolution* |
| Shelby | "Kings Mountain: Letters of Colonel Isaac Shelby," ed. J. G. Roulhac Hamilton, *Journal of Southern History* 4, no. 3 (August 1938) |
| Smith | Paul H. Smith, *Loyalists and Redcoats: A Study in British Revolutionary Policy* (1964; reprint, New York: W. W. Norton, 1972) |
| Swager | Christine R. Swager, *Musgrove Mill Historic Site* (Infinity Publishing, 2013) |
| Watlington | Patricia Watlington, *The Partisan Spirit: Kentucky Politics, 1779–1782* (New York: Atheneum, 1972) |
| WHS | Wisconsin Historical Society |
| Williams | Williams' Report, in Graves (above) |
| Wrobel | Sylvia Wrobel and George Gilder, *Isaac Shelby: Kentucky's First Governor and Hero of Three Wars* (Danville, KY: Cumberland Press, 1974) |

PREFACE

1. Swager, vi.
2. Collins, 237–38.

CHAPTER 1. "PACK OF BEGGARS"

1.. For the document, see William Moultrie, *Memoirs of the American Revolution,* 2 vols. (1802; reprint, Bedford, MA: Applewood Books, n.d.), 2: 386–88. For the

British invasion, the fall of Charleston and the surrender of an American army, and the British advance into the Back Country, see *GCH*, Chs. 3–7. This chapter is based on, and is a shorter version of, the Prologue in *RTC*.

2. Jim Piecuch, "The Southern Theater: Britain's Last Chance for Victory," in *Theaters of the American Revolution*, ed. James Kirby Martin and David L. Preston (Yardley, PA: Westholme Press, 2017), 90–91 for the quotations.

3. Piecuch, ibid., 92; Cornwallis to Balfour, July 3, 1780, Brown to Cornwallis, June 28, 1780, Cornwallis to Brown, July 17, 1780, *CP*, 1: 245, 272–75; Stuart to Germain, August 23, 1776, quoted in James H. O'Donnell III, *Southern Indians in the American Revolution* (Knoxville: University of Tennessee Press, 1973), 48–50. For a discussion of the Indian danger to the Southern Back Country, see *RTC*, 253–57.

4. For my discussion of such fiction, see *RTC*, 20, and for Nathanael Greene's attempt to raise a black regiment, 272–73, 292–94.

5. For a brief but highly informative discussion of Sir Henry Clinton, see John Ferling, *Winning Independence: The Decisive Years of the Revolutionary War, 1778–1781* (New York: Bloomsbury, 2021) 554–59, and *passim* (see index under Clinton, Henry; Cornwallis, Charles; Germain, George, for further discussions of the British move South). For Cornwallis' adventures in South and North Carolina, see *GCH* and *RTC*.

6. Clinton to Cornwallis, May 29, 1780, Cornwallis to Clinton, June 2, 1780, *CP*, 1: 54–55; Allaire, 496–99. For brief but authoritative discussions of provincial regulars, see the essays by Thomas B. Allen and Todd W. Braisted in *Loyalist Corps*, 9–19. I am indebted to Scott Withrow for the location of Keowee and information regarding the town, and to Dennis Chastain for the mileage.

7. Balfour to Cornwallis, June 7, 1780, June 12, 1780, June 24, 1780, *CP*, 1: 78, 84, 239.

8. *Loyalist Corps*, 27–29.

9. Allaire, 491; Charles Stedman, *The History of the Origin, Progress, and Termination of the American War*, 2 vols. (London, 1794), 2: 183; for the identity and travail of Ann Fayssoux, see C. Leon Harris and Charles B. Baxley, "Tarleton Tightens the Noose Around Charlestown Neck: Biggin Bridge, April 14, 1780," *SCAR*, 18, no. 2 (November 29, 2021), 22–23; Cornwallis to Tarleton, April 25, 1780, *CP*, 1: 25; Nicholas Penny, ed., *Reynolds* (New York: Abrams, 1986), 377–78; Farrington, *Diary*, 3: 832, quoted in the *Oxford Dictionary of National Biography*, authored by the British historian Stephen Conway; for Tarleton in Virginia late in the war and his postwar years, see *GCH*, 386–88.

10. For a full description of the Waxhaws action, including quotations with citations in this and the two following paragraphs, see *GCH*, 80–85; for a revisionist version by a noted historian, see Jim Piecuch, *The Blood Be Upon Your Head, Tarleton and the Myth of Buford's Massacre: The Battle of the Waxhaws, May 29, 1780* (Lugoff, SC: Southern Campaigns of the American Revolution Press, 2010); for

Tarleton's background, *GCH,* 58–60. Strong evidence that a massacre happened is in *RTC,* 21–22.

11. Banastre Tarleton, *History of the Campaigns of 1780 and 1781 in the Provinces of North America* (London, 1787), 30–31.

12. John C. Dann, *Revolution Remembered: Eyewitness Accounts of the War for Independence* (Chicago: University of Chicago Press, 1980), 202.

13. *Journal of . . . Archibald Campbell, Esquire, Lieut. Colo. of His Majesty's 71st Regimt. 1778,* ed. Colin Campbell (Darien, GA: Ashantilly Press, 1981), 4–7; Prevost to Lord Germain, March 5, 1779, *DAR,*17:77.

14. For the Back Country population estimate of two-thirds to three-quarters, see Robert M. Weir, *Colonial South Carolina: A History* (Millwood, NY: KTO Press, 1983), 209. If we use the two-thirds figure, there were at least 48,840 whites in the Back Country. For the white and black populations in 1775, see Walter Edgar, *South Carolina: A History* (Columbia: University of South Carolina Press, 1998), Table 5.2, 78; Cornwallis to John Harris Cruger, August 5, 1780, *CP,* 1: 256; Clinton to Cornwallis, May 20, 1780, *CP,* 1, 49; John Wilson, *Encounters on a March Through Georgia in 1779: The Maps and Memorandums of John Wilson, Engineer, 71st Highland Regiment,* ed. Robert Scott Davis (Sylvania, GA: Partridge Pond Press, 1986), 8.

15. Robert Gray, "Colonel Robert Gray's Observations on the War in the Carolinas," *South Carolina Historical and Genealogical Magazine* 11, no. 3 (July 1910), 140, 148; Lambert, 321.

16. Robert L. Meriwether, *The Expansion of South Carolina, 1729–1765* (Kingsport, TN: Southern Publishers, 1940), 118; Charles Woodmason, *The Carolina Back Country on the Eve of the Revolution: The Journal and Other Writings of Charles Woodmason Anglican Itinerant,* Richard J. Hooker, ed. (Chapel Hill: University of North Carolina Press, 1953), 12; Collins, 292.

17. Meriwether, *The Expansion of South Carolina,* 118–19.

18. Meriwether, *The Expansion of South Carolina,* 119–20 for the commander's opinion and the quotation; the "Riff-Raff" quote is in Tom Hatley, *The Dividing Paths: Cherokees and South Carolinians Through the Era of Revolution* (New York: Oxford University Press, 1993), 146; the "Pack of Beggars" quote is in Woodmason, *The Carolina Backcountry on the Eve of the Revolution,* 273, and Woodmason's rant about the Scotch-Irish is on 60–61; the other opinion of the Scotch-Irish, July 1765, was by Robert Jones, North Carolina Attorney General, which came to me courtesy of John Allison; Washington's quote is in Dorothy Twohig, "The Making of George Washington," and Warren Hofstra, "'A Parcel of Barbarian's and an Uncooth Set of People': Settlers and Settlement of the Shenandoah Valley," in Hofstra, ed., *George Washington and the Virginia Backcountry* (Madison, WI: Madison House Publishers, 1998), 15–16, 88; Jay to Jefferson, December 14 , 1786, *The Papers of Thomas Jefferson* (Princeton: Princeton University Press, 1950– ), 10: 598–99.

19. For details on the American Volunteers, see *Loyalist Corps*, 21–22. For the quotations and Ferguson's scorched earth recommendations, see *GCH*, 200–202.
20. Clinton's instructions to Ferguson, May 22, 1780, *CP*, 1: 103–5, with quotations on 105.
21. Prevost to Clinton, March 1, 1779, *DAR*, 17: 69; courtesy of Jim Piecuch, "The Loyalist Exodus from South Carolina in 1778," unpublished paper, Society for Military History Conference, April 2008.
22. Ferguson to Cornwallis, May 30, 1780, Cornwallis to Ferguson, June 2, 1780, *CP*, 1: 99–102.
23. Balfour to Cornwallis, May 30, 1780, *CP*, 1: 74. Note that the editor of *The Cornwallis Papers* explained that Balfour's use of the word "doubt" was "in the archaic sense of 'fear.'"
24. Cornwallis to Clinton, June 30, 1780, *CP*, 1: 161–63.
25. For a discussion of the action at Ramsour's Mill, see *GCH*, 106–10.
26. Cornwallis to Innes, June 16, 1780, *CP*, 1: 119; William Richardson Davie, *The Revolutionary War Sketches of William R. Davie*, ed. Blackwell P. Robinson (Raleigh: North Carolina Division of Archives and History, 1976), 8.
27. Cornwallis to Clinton, August 23, 1780, *CP*, 2: 17.
28. For the Battle of Huck's Defeat, see Michael C. Scoggins, *The Day It Rained Militia: Huck's Defeat and the Revolution in the South Carolina Back Country May–July 1780* (The History Press, 2005). For the number of actions, see Terry W. Lipscomb, *Battles, Skirmishes, and Actions of the American Revolution in South Carolina* (South Carolina Department of Archives & History, 1991), 7–8. Lipscomb's work is now more than thirty years old, yet I still find it useful. I am aware of and have a copy of John C. Parker, Jr., *Parker's Guide to the Revolutionary War in South Carolina: Battles, Skirmishes & Murders*, 2nd ed. (Infinity Publishing, 2013). In his "Chronological Order of Actions," Parker has included murders and other incidents, including a possible rape, that, in my opinion, do not fit the description of actions. Although *Parker's Guide* is a fine work of wide research, and is especially valuable for locations, I continue to largely rely on Lipscomb.
29. David Ramsay, *A History of the Revolution in South Carolina from a British Province to an Independent State*, 2 vols. (Trenton, NJ: Isaac Collins, 1785), 2: 275; William Moultrie, *Memoirs of the American Revolution* (1802; reprint, Bedford, MA: Applewood Books, n.d.), 2: 203; Sumter to Greene, December 19, 1781, *PNG*, 10: 81.
30. Collins, 245–47.
31. Davie, *The Revolutionary War Sketches of William R. Davie*, 13; for a discussion of the problems with militia and citations, see *GCH*, 366–68.
32. Rawdon to Clinton, March 23, 1781, *The American Rebellion: Sir Henry Clinton's Narrative of his Campaigns, 1775–1782, with an Appendix of Original Documents*, ed. William B. Willcox (New Haven: Yale University Press, 1954), 501.
33. See in www.southerncampaigns.org/pen, Joseph Alexander (S15355), Bailey Anderson (S30826), William Black (S9730), Ralph Cassell (R1791), Daniel

Chandler (S32175), Pharaoh Cobb ((S1657), John Collins ((S8248), Edward Cox ((S3170), Ebenezer Fain (R3421), David Golightly (S18888), William Goodlett (W8857), Samuel Hammond (S21807), Jacob Holman ((R5165), Joseph Hughes (S31764), William Kenedy (S2965), Moses Lindsey (S4551), Michael Massengill ((S1687), Joseph McJunkin (S18118), John Mills (S9024), Hugh Moore (W8473), Levi Mote ((S7245), Matthew Patton (S18153), Alexander Peden (S21417), Samuel Peden (S30649), Henry Pettit (W5528), Valentine Sevier (W6012, Gilbert Shaw (W3876), William Smith (W22272), Landon Farrow (W21088), Henry Story ((S32537), Lewis Taylor (S1728), Andrew Willson (R11674), William Young (W10008); George Washington to Orange County Committee of Public Safety, July 14, 1776, *The Papers of George Washington*, ed. W. W. Abbot and Dorothy Twohig (Charlottesville: University Press of Virginia, 1993), 5: 314.

34. Pension Application of William Kenedy (S2965), and Pension Application of John Mills (S9024), in www.southerncampaigns.org/pen.

35. Pension Application of William Wilbanks (R11508), in www.southerncampaigns.org/pen.

36. *GCH*, 112; Collins, 245–47; Allaire, 508.

37. For the number of actions, Lipscomb, *Battles, Skirmishes, and Actions of the American Revolution in South Carolina*, 3–24; Cornwallis to Alexander Leslie, November 12, 1780, *Correspondence of Charles, First Marquis Cornwallis*, 3 vols., ed. Charles Ross (London: John Murray, 1859), 1: 69; Balfour to Cornwallis, November 5, 1780, *CP*, 3: 65; Cruger to Cornwallis, November 23, 1780, quoted in Jim Piecuch, *Three Peoples, One King: Loyalists, Indians, and Slaves in the Revolutionary South, 1775–1781* (Columbia: University of South Carolina Press, 2008), 233.

38. "Gray's Observations on the War in the Carolinas," 144.

39. Cornwallis to Tarleton, November 23, 1780, *CP*, 3: 342.

40. Graves, 102–3.

41. Swager, 27.

42. Dann, *Revolution Remembered*, 184.

43. Kevin J. Weddle, *The Compleat Victory: Saratoga and the American Revolution* (New York: Oxford University Press, 2021), 389.

44. For a description of Gates' background, my opinion of him, and the Battle of Camden, see *GCH*, Chapter 11, "A Hero Takes Charge," and Chapter 12, "The Battle of Camden."

## CHAPTER 2. THE COLONELS

1. Clarke eventually learned to sign his letters with a crude E. Others wrote his letters and read to him incoming correspondence.

2. College football fans will recognize that I borrowed these words from the famous University of Alabama football coach, Paul "Bear" Bryant. When asked by

a reporter what he looked for in a player, the "Bear" replied, "I like 'em Agile, Mobile, and Hostile."

3. Elizabeth Lichtenstein Johnston, *Recollections of a Georgia Loyalist* (Spartanburg, SC: Reprint Company, 1972), 45; Shelby, 372; Cornwallis to Balfour, November 25, 1780, *CP*, 3, 89. There is no scholarly biography of Clarke. A book that purports to be, *Hero of the Hornet's Nest: A Biography of Elijah Clarke, 1733–1799*, by Louise Frederick Hays, is a mix of biography and fiction, and I have chosen not to read it for fear of repeating dubious stories. My chief source for Clarke is an excellent article by Robert Scott Davis, "Elijah Clarke: Georgia's Partisan Titan," *SCAR*, 4: 1–3 (January–March, 2007), 38–40. His name appears in writings as Clarke or Clark. I have chosen to follow Professor Davis' lead.

4. *CP*, 1: 34; William Shakespeare, *King John*, ed. E. A. J. Honigmann (London: Methuen, 1954), 29; Habersham quoted in Edward J. Cashin, "From Creeks to Crackers," in *The Southern Colonial Backcountry: Interdisciplinary Perspectives on Frontier Communities*, ed. David Colin Crass et al. (Knoxville: University of Tennessee Press, 1998), 69; *New York Daily News*, February 5, 2022.

5. *South Carolina and American General Gazette* (Charleston), September 27, 1780, p. 2, c. 3. Quoted in Robert Scott Davis, "Lessons from Kettle Creek: Patriotism and Loyalism at Askance on the Southern Frontier" (March 22, 2006), 28.

6. Davis, "Lessons from Kettle Creek." The Chowanoac Indians lived in northeastern North Carolina when the whites arrived. By 1751, they ceased to exist as a tribe.

7. Descriptions of the Battle of Alligator Bridge are in Cashin, *King's Ranger*, 77–79, and Martha C. Searcy, *The Georgia–Florida Contest in the American Revolution, 1776–1778* (Tuscaloosa: University of Alabama Press, 1985), 144–45, 150; for the quotation on Brown. *Loyalist Corps*, 38, 53–54.

8. Searcy, *Georgia–Florida Contest*, 10.

9. Dooly to Samuel Elbert, February 16, 1779, *SCAR* 3, nos. 2, 3 (February 2006), 39; Pickens to Henry Lee, August 28, 1811, Draper Mss, 1 VV 107, Wisconsin Historical Society; for the British invasion of Georgia, a description of the Battle of Kettle Creek, and the run-up to it and aftermath, see *RTC*, 4–9.

10. Cruger to Officer commanding at Camden, August 4, 1780, *CP*, I, 257; Pension application of Ebenezer Fain (R3421R) in www.southerncampaigns.org/ pen.

11. Allaire, 502–3.

12. Ferguson to Cornwallis, August 9, 1780, *CP*, 1: 302; Allaire, 503; Shelby, *Letters*, 371; Draper, 94; *GCH*, 138–39; Loyalist Corps, 35 for Dunlop's previous service (note also that both Ferguson and Allaire spelled his name as Dunlap); *Captured at King's Mountain: The Journal of Uzal Johnson, A Loyalist Surgeon*, ed. Wade S. Kolbe III and Robert M. Weir (Columbia: University of South Carolina Press, 2011), 24.

13. Allaire, 503. Dr. Ross was probably William Ross, according to the editors of Johnson's *Journal*, Notes for August 10, 1780, 91.

14. Quotations in Wrobel, 9,10.

15. For the first quotation, Glenn F. Williams, *Dunmore's War: The Last Conflict of America's Colonial Era* (Yardley, PA: Westholme Publishing, 2018), 288. I highly recommend this book. It is the definitive history of the war and the reasons that led to it. The second quotation is in Wrobel, 17.

16. This paragraph and the following are based on discussions in *RTC*, 255–56, and John Buchanan, *Jackson's Way: Andrew Jackson and the People of the Western Waters* (New York: John Wiley & Sons, 2001), 28–31.

17. *RTC*, 255 and citations; *History of Tennessee: Making of a State* (Boston: Houghton Mifflin, 1888), 44.

18. *History of Tennessee*, 55.

19. Pension application of Pharaoh Cobb (S1657). www.southerncampaigns. org/pen; Nisbet Balfour to Cornwallis, September 22, 1780, *CP*, 2: 94.

20. Graves, 10–13. Unless otherwise indicated, my description of Williams' life prior to Musgrove's Mill is based on Graves.

21. Graves, 11.

22. Lindley S. Butler, ed., *The Narrative of Col. David Fanning* (Davidson, NC: Briarpatch Press, 1981), 31.

23. Graves, 78.

24. First quotation in Ron Andrew, Jr., *The Life and Times of Andrew Pickens: Revolutionary War Hero, American Founder* (Chapel Hill: University of North Carolina Press, 2017), 88; Pickens to Lee, August 28, 1811, Draper Mss., 1 VV 107, WHS.

25. John Allison to John Buchanan, January 22, 2022; Scoggins, 83; McJunkin's Narrative in Graves, 295; Rutledge to Delegates, September 20, 1780, *South Carolina Historical and Genealogical Magazine*, 17, no. 4 (October 1916), 136–39; Cornwallis to Ferguson, October 1, 1780, *CP*, 2, 158–59.

26. Graves, 82; McJunkin's Narrative in Graves, 299.

## CHAPTER 3. "DEAD MEN LAY THICK ON THE GROUND"

1. For the number of riders, Williams Report, 196–97; for the quotation, Shelby, 371–72; for the British belief that only Sumter's force was engaged against them, Ferguson to Ross, August 19, 1780, *CP*, 2, 145; for "Sumter's surprise" at Fishing Creek, GCH, 173–76. The scholar's description of pre-modern communications is in Rosemary Salomone, *The Rise of English: Global Politics and the Power of Language* (New York: Oxford University Press, 2022), 6.

2. Draper, 313.

3. Joseph Hughes (S31764), William Kenedy (S2965), John Mills (S9024), Alexander Peden (S21417), in www.southerncampaigns.org/pen.

4. This paragraph is slightly rewritten from one I wrote almost thirty years ago and can be found in *GCH*, 61.

5. Shelby, 372; Major Joseph McJunkin in Graves, 300.

6. Shelby, 372; Hammond, 102 (Hammond is in Johnston, 519–22, but more

accessible for the reader in Graves, 102–4, n. 208); Graves, 227, 111; for Ferguson camped at Culbertson's and his march thereafter, see Johnson, 24; for Ferguson camped at Winn's plantation, see Ferguson to Alexander Ross, August 19, 1780, *CP*, 2, 144–45, and Johnson, 25ff, Allaire, 504–5, Chesney, 23; Hiatt, 26. According to Draper, 104–5, Ferguson was camped at Fair Forest Shoal, three or four miles from the Rebels' route of march, but as usual he did not give a source, and his statement is negated by four eyewitnesses: Ferguson, Johnson, Allaire, and Chesney, who all agree on Ferguson's location at Winn's plantation on the night the Rebels rode to Musgrove's Mill.

7. Shelby, 372. Shelby wrote that the newly arrived force consisted of 600 regulars, which was wildly off the mark; I have accepted Hammond, 103, for the number of regulars, and specifically for the South Carolina Royalists, Innes' letter to Cornwallis cited in n. 11, below.

8. Howe to Innes, January 29, 1777, Boston Public Library, Rare Books and Manuscripts, Misc. Acc.1328, courtesy of Todd Braisted; "Notes," Innes, for his background; Cornwallis to Clinton, May 7, 1780, *CP*, I: 20, for Innes' assignments; Chesney, 110, for the negative description of Innes, as quoted by the editor of Chesney's *Journal*, Bobby Gilmer Moss.

9. Innes to Cornwallis, *CP*, 1: 111–12.

10. Balfour to Cornwallis, June 27, 1780, *CP*, 1, 243; for Fraser's background, "Notes," Fraser, Hiatt, 28 n36, and *CP*, 1, 243 n.11 for his postwar history.

11. Innes to Cornwallis, September 5, 1781, *CP*, 2: 181 for the number of South Carolina Royalists and recruits; Lambert, 71–72 for the recruitment of the regiment in Florida; Cruger to Cornwallis, August 11, 1780, *CP*, 1, 260; Roderick Mackenzie, *Strictures on Lt. Col. Tarleton's History of the Campaigns of 1780 and 1781 in the Southern Provinces of North America* (London, 1781), 12; Innes to Cornwallis, September 5, 1780, *CP*, 2, 181; Innes to Cornwallis, July 28, 1780, *CP*, 1, 268.

12. Brian Robson, "British Forces in the Battle of Musgrove's Mill: A Breakdown of the Loyalist Militia and Provincial Regulars from the First Encampment to the Battle," unpublished paper, n.d. (circa 2011?). Robson was the historian and park manager at the Musgrove Mill Historic Site. The paper was most helpful in estimating the size of the entire Loyalist force.

13. *Loyalist Corps*, 32–33.

14. Information on this unit is in Todd W. Braisted, *Grand Forage, 1778: The Battleground Around New York City* (Yardley, PA: Westholme Publishing, 2016), 50, 152–54, and Braisted's website, royalprovincial.com.

15. Williams, 196–97; Hammond, 103; Cruger to the officer commanding at Camden, August 4, 1780, *CP*, 1, 257; Lambert, 300–301, for Clary remaining in America; *The Narrative of Col. David Fanning*, ed. Lindley S. Butler (Davidson, NC: Briarpatch Press, 1981), 32. The Indian line, established in 1761, was the boundary between Cherokees and South Carolina settlers. It was about thirty-five miles west of Ninety Six.

16. Innes to Cornwallis, August 16, 1780, giving the date of his departure from Ninety Six and the date of Cornwallis' August 13, 1780, letter, which is not extant, ordering Innes to join Ferguson, and Cruger to Cornwallis, August 16, 1780, indicating that the purpose of Innes' march is to join Ferguson, *CP*, 2, 168–69; enclosure in Cruger to Clary, August 9, 1780, *CP*, 1, 264–65; Ferguson to Alexander Ross, August 19, 1781, *CP*, 2, 140; for the location of Lisles Ford, Wade S. Kolb III and Robert M. Weir, *The Journal of Uzal Johnson: A Loyalist Surgeon* (Columbia: University of South Carolina Press, 2011), 93.

17. Shelby, 372; Hammond, 103.

18. Graves, 228; Hammond, 103.

19. Logan, 2: 427–28. Logan also wrote that Lieutenant Colonel John Harris Cruger was there and wanted to wait for the patrol's return but that Innes prevailed. Colonel Cruger was *not* at Musgrove's Mill. He was at Ninety Six. Besides that, if Cruger had been there, as Innes' superior the decision was his to make.

20. Fanning, *Narrative*, 32.

21. "Old Indian field" is in Logan, 2: 427, and 434 for no breastworks reported; Hammond, 103; Williams, 197, for the length of the Rebel line; Shelby, 372; and author's visit to the ridge where the battle began.

22. Hammond, 103; Williams, 197.

23. Hammond, 103; Williams, 197.

24. Hammond, 103–4.

25. Hammond (40, 50), 103–4; Shelby (70), 372; Williams (80), 197.

26. Hammond, 104; Shelby, 372; Draper, 108.

27. The On-Line Institute for Advanced Loyalist Studies, "A History of the 3rd Battalion, New Jersey Volunteers" (August 26, 2003), 6; McLaurin to Nisbet Balfour, August 22, 1780, Thomas Addis Emmett Collection, Manuscripts and Archives Division, New York Public Library, Miscellaneous Manuscripts (microfilm); Innes to Cornwallis, September 5, 1780, *CP*, II, 181.

28. Henry Lumpkin, *From Savannah to Yorktown: The American Revolution in the South* (New York: Paragon House Publishers, 1981), 100, for the de Peyster quote; Hammond, 104; Shelby, 372.

29. Draper, 109; Swager, 61–62, for the Clary family's role.

30. Williams, 197; Fanning, 32; Hammond, 104.

31. Graves, 197, 229; Shelby, 372.

32. Casualty figures for Bunker Hill: Paul D. Lockhart, *The Whites of Their Eyes* (New York: HarperCollins, 2011), 306–7 (also for the quotation); Richard M. Ketchum, *The Battle for Bunker Hill* (Garden City, NY: Doubleday, 1962), 121, 144–45, 147; *Encyclopaedia Britannica*, 14th edition (1929); *Encyclopedia of American History*, Revised and Enlarged Edition, ed. Richard B. Morris (1961); *An Encyclopedia of Battles*, ed. David Eggenberger (New York: Dover Publications, 1985).

33. Roderick Mackenzie, *Strictures of Lt. Col. Tarleton's History*, 24–26, for the numbers of provincial officers present and wounded (we know the names of six,

which are listed in Appendix B, British/Tory Order of Battle); Graves, 197, for Williams' numbers, and see also 115, n. 239 for figures purportedly by the staff of the Musgrove Mill Historic Site that claim the Loyalist wounded numbered ninety, but according to the present staff of the site those numbers probably were not produced by the staff and therefore I do not accept them; Edward Doyle (S32216), www.southerncampaigns.org/pen; Cruger to Cornwallis, August 23, 1780, *CP*, 2, 170; Cornwallis to Clinton, August 23, 1780, *CP*, 2, 16–17.
34. Cornwallis to Cruger, August 24, 1780, *CP*, 2, 169.
35. Shelby, 373; McKeen Greene pension application (W7561) in www.southerncampaigns.org/pen.
36. Stewart to Cornwallis, September 9, 1781, *Documents of the American Revolution, 1770–1783* (Colonial Office Series), 21 vols., ed. K. G. Davies (Shannon: Irish University Press, 1972–1981), 20: 226–29; for Greene's siege of Ninety Six and the Battle of Eutaw Springs, see *RTC*, Chapters 6 & 10.
37. Ferguson to Alexander Ross, August 19, 1780, *CP*, 2, 144, acknowledging the order to move against Sumter; Johnson, entry of August 19, 25; Chesney, 24; Allaire, 24, contains almost word for word the information in Johnson.
38. Graves, 300; Shelby, 372–73.
39. Shelby, 373; Hammond, 104. For the Battle of Long Island, see John Buchanan, *The Road to Valley Forge: How Washington Built the Army That Won the Revolution* (New York: John Wiley & Sons, 2004), 43–119. For the effort to supplant Washington as commander in chief, see Mark Edward Lender, *Cabal: The Plot Against General Washington* (Yardley, PA: Westholme Publishing, 2019).

CHAPTER 4. "THIS LITTLE AFFAIR, TRIFLING AS IT MAY SEEM"

1. The first quotation is in Cashin, 120, in his otherwise excellent book on Thomas Brown. Cornwallis to Clinton, December 3, 1780, *CP*, 3: 24.
2. Cruger to Cornwallis, September 23, 1780, *CP*, 2: 192; Ferguson to Cornwallis, September 28, 1780, October 1, 1780, *CP*, 2: 159, 162; Allaire, 509; Johnson, 30. Will Graves informed me that an even closer landmark for the location of James Step's is the intersection of North Carolina Highway 1326 (Coxe Road) with White Oak Creek, a tributary of the Greene River.
3. Balfour to Cornwallis, June 27, 1780, Cornwallis to Balfour, July 3, 1780, *CP*, 1: 242, 245. Sugar Creek was just north of Musgrove's Mill.
4. Cornwallis to Ferguson, August 5, 1780, *CP*, 1: 301; Ferguson to Ross, August 19, 1780, *CP*, 2: 141; "cursed nest" was Balfour's term in Balfour to Cornwallis, September 22, 1780, *CP*, 2: 94.
5. Shelby, 372–73, and slightly different in his narrative in Graves, 231; Robert Henry, *Narrative of the Battle of Cowan's Ford . . . and Narrative of the Battle of King's Mountain by Captain David Vance* (Greensboro, NC: D. Schenck, 1891), 18. When he wrote "fled to their country," Shelby meant that Charles McDowell and his Back Country partisans had gone over the mountains to where the Over Mountain Men lived.

6. Draper, 169, and his citations.

7. Tarleton to Henry Haldane, December 24, 1780, quoted in Franklin and Mary Wickwire, *Cornwallis: The American Adventure* (Boston: Houghton Mifflin, 1970), 258.

8. Henry Clinton, *American Rebellion*, ed. William B. Willcox (New Haven: Yale University Press, 1954), 226.

EPILOGUE: WHAT HAPPENED TO THE COLONELS?

1. Steven J. Rauch, "'An Ill-Timed and Premature Insurrection': The First Siege at Augusta, Georgia, September 14–18, 1780," *SCAR*, 2, no. 9 (September 2005), 4, for the number of men Clarke raised and the Burnett quotation; Cruger to Cornwallis, September 28, 1780, *CP*, 2, 194; Cashin, 27–28.

2. *Journal of . . . Archibald Campbell, Esquire, Lieut. Colo. of His Majesty's 71st Regiment, 1778*, ed. Colin Campbell (Darien, GA: Ashantilly Press, 1981), 54–55; Brown's return in Cruger to Cornwallis, September 15, 1780, *CP*, 2, 187; William Bartram, *The Travels of William Bartram: Naturalist's Edition*, ed. Francis Harper (1958; reprint, Athens: University of Georgia Press, 1998), 200.

3. Davis, 38; Brown to Cruger, September 15, 1780, *CP*, 2: 189.

4. Cruger to Cornwallis, December 15, 1780, December 16, 1780, *CP*, 2: 187–88.

5. Cashin, *The King's Ranger*, 113–18; Cruger to Cornwallis, December 19, 1780, *CP*, 2, 190.

6. Cruger to Balfour, September 19, 1780, *CP*, II, 103; Hugh McCall, *The History of Georgia* (1784; reprint, Atlanta: A. B. Caldwell, 1909), 486–87; Rauch, "An Ill-Timed and Premature Insurrection," 13; Cruger to Cornwallis, September 23 & September 28, 1780, *CP*, 2, 192, 194.

7. Rauch, "An Ill-Timed and Premature Insurrection," 13, for the number in the refugee column; Cruger to Cornwallis, September 28, 1780, *CP*, 2, 194 for the quotations and Cruger's refugee number.

8. Pickens to Greene, April 8, 1781, *PNG*, 8: 70–71.

9. See *GCH*, 248–5, for a description of the action at Fishdam Ford.

10. See *GCH*, 251–59 for a description of the Battle of Blackstock's.

11. Cornwallis to Tarleton, November 11, 1780, *CP*, 3: 336.

12. Tarleton to Cornwallis, November 21, 1780, *CP*, 3: 340.

13. Banastre Tarleton, *A History of the Campaigns of 1780 and 1781 in the Southern Provinces of North America* (London, 1787), 178; Tarleton to Cornwallis, November 21, 1780, *CP*, 3: 340.

14. Pension Applications of John Henderson (R4869), David H. Thurmond (S32010), Levin Watson (S7797), www.southerncampaigns.org.pen

15. For an excellent study of the siege and its consequences, see Steven J. Rauch, "The Second Siege of Augusta, Georgia," *SCAR*, 3, no. 6–8 (June–July–August 2006).

16. Lee to Greene, June 4, 1781, Greene to Clarke, May 29, 1781, *PNG*, 8: 346, 324–25.

17. Thomas Taylor to John Wesley, February 28, 1782, quoted in Cashin, *King's Ranger*, 137.

18. Davis, 39. My discussion of Clarke's postwar career is to a great degree based on Professor Robert Scott Davis's excellent article "Elijah Clarke: Georgia's Partisan Titan." See Davis in Abbreviations for the full citation.

19. Clarke to Governor George Matthews, September 24, 1787, in George White, *Historical Collections of Georgia* (Pudney & Russell, 1854), 672–73.

20. Michael Morris, "Dreams of Glory, Schemes of Empire: The Plan to Liberate Spanish Florida," *Georgia Historical Quarterly*, 87, no. 1 (Spring 2006), 7, 9.

21. My chief source for Genet is the splendid work by Carol Berkin, *A Sovereign People: The Crises of the 1790's and the Birth of American Nationalism* (New York: Basic Books, 2017), Part II, "The Genet Affair," 81–150, with the quotation on 134.

22. Davis, 39.

23. Robert J. Alderson, Jr., "Entangled Borderlands: The 1794 Projected French Invasion of Spanish East Florida and Atlantic History," *Florida Historical Quarterly*, 8, no. 1 (Summer 2009), 68, 75; Bridges, 12–13, and the quotation.

24. For a discussion of the Treaty of New York, see John Buchanan, *Jackson's Way: Andrew Jackson and the People of the Western Waters* (New York: John Wiley & Sons, 2001), 101–4, and citations, especially Francis Paul Prucha, *American Indian Treaties*.

25. Flournoy to Seagrove, October 5, 1793, *ASP, IA,* II, 416–17; *Augusta Chronicle*, January 4, 1794, quoted in Bridges, 13.

26. Bridges, 11; James Seagrove to Edward Telfair, October 3, 1793, *ASP, IA,* II, 412.

27. Bridges, 14–15; *ASP, IA,* II; James Seagrove to the Governor of Georgia, 487.

28. Bridges, 15; Freeman to the Secretary of War, September 29, 1794, *ASP, IA,* II, 500.

29. Freeman to Secretary of War, September 29, 1794, *ASP, IA,* II, 500; Bridges, 16.

30. Bridges, 16; Davis, 39.

31. The words are by Robert Scott Davis, "Lessons from Kettle Creek," 58, n.71, paraphrasing Clarke to Dr. McDonald, December 9, 1794, Draper MSS, Georgia, Alabama, and South Carolina Papers (Reel 60, 1V, 11).

32. Lawrence Babits to John Buchanan, August 1, 2021. Babits is the author of *Devil of a Whipping: The Battle of Cowpens*, the definitive history of the battle.

33. The exchanges can be followed in *RTC*, 164–65, 216–17, 263, and in the following correspondence: Greene to Shelby, June 22, 1781, Shelby to Greene, July 2, 1781, August 3, 1781, Sevier to Greene, August 6, 1781, Marion to Greene, November 2, 1781, *PNG*, 8: 439, 482; 9: 129, 143, 522.

34. Marion to Greene, November 18, 1781, November 27, 1781, *PNG*, 9: 590, 632.

35. My chief sources for Shelby's postwar career in Kentucky are Watlington, *The Partisan Spirit*; and Wrobel, *Isaac Shelby*. It should be noted that Watlington is a sound, scholarly work, but Wrobel should be used with caution, as it is often wrong on details, especially his Revolutionary War career. And, incredibly, there is no index. Isaac Shelby awaits a major, scholarly biography.

36. Watlington, 43–44, 59, 148–49.

37. For readers who wish to pursue the "conspiracy," see Arthur Preston Whitaker, *The Spanish American Frontier, 1783–1795: The Westward Movement and the Spanish Retreat in the Mississippi Valley* (1927; reprint, Lincoln: University of Nebraska Press, 1969), passim. An excellent up-to-date study of the whole range of crises facing the federal government in the 1790s is Carol Berkin, *A Sovereign People*.

38. Quoted in Watlington, 186–87.

39. Watlington, 77.

40. Quoted in Henderson, 453.

41. Henderson, 453–57, 463; Berkin, 43.

42. Henderson, 461.

43. Berkin, 43–44.

44. Quimby, I: 134–35, and 134–40 for the consequences.

45. Quimby, I: 102–3; Wrobel, 116.

46. Wrobel, 116–19; Quimby, I: 259–60.

47. Quimby, I: 274–75.

48. Quimby, I: 278.

49. Quimby, I: 286.

50. Graves, 329.

51. This section is based on William T. Graves, *Back Country Revolutionary: James Williams (1740–1780) with Source Documents* (Lugoff, SC: Southern Campaigns of the American Revolution Press, 2012), 80–99. My discussion of the controversy is in *GCH*, 217, 220–21—and I take it all back.

52. Rutledge to Delegates, September 20, 1780, *South Carolina Historical and Genealogical Magazine*, 17, no. 4 (Oct. 1916), 136–39; Cornwallis to Ferguson, October 1, 1780, *CP*, 2: 158–59.

53. Anne King Gregorie, *Thomas Sumter* (Columbia, SC: R. L. Bryan, 1931), 97.

54. Graves, 299.

55. Ibid.

56. Graves, Ch. 8, "Confrontation with Hill," 80–99.

57. Graves, 235, n.350, and Appendix 20, 326–36.

# Acknowledgments

I AM INDEBTED TO Mark Edward Lender and James Kirby Martin for their careful reading of the manuscript and sage advice. They sharpened my thinking and made it a better book. Christine Swager, whose own book on Musgrove's Mill was most helpful, sent me a box containing all of her research materials, and also read the manuscript with, as always, her keen eye. William T. Graves' excellent book on James Williams, *Backcountry Revolutionary*, goes far beyond the subject and was a critical source. How can I repay John Allison, Charles Baxley, Brett Bennett, and Ed Forte, for taking time out of their busy lives to give me a walking tour of the battlefield? And here I must stress that it was John Allison's archaeological endeavors that pinpointed the ridge a mile and a half from Musgrove's Ford where the Rebels awaited the Tory onslaught. Charles Baxley and John Allison also helpfully critiqued the manuscript, and Ed Forte kindly allowed me to copy his valuable research papers. I am grateful to Todd Braisted for setting me straight on Loyalist officers and units. Scott Withrow and Dennis Chastain were most helpful on geography and distance. I also thank Dawn Weaver, Manager of Musgrove Mill Historic Site, and the Sites Interpretive Ranger, Mark Stanford, for their assistance. Kirsten Carleton at the 268-year-old treasure that is only four blocks from my apartment, the New York Society Library, chartered in 1754 by George II, secured for me some obscure sources through interlibrary loans. And I am indebted beyond measure to the superb professionals at Westholme Publishing: Bruce H. Franklin, publisher; Noreen O'Connor, editor; and Tracy Dungan, map maker. If I have forgotten anybody, *mea culpa!*

# Index